Torah, Ice Hockey, _and_ Astrophysics

W0010543

Ira J. Kalet

ISBN: 978-1-09834-626-3 (softcover)
ISBN: 978-1-09834-627-0 (eBook)

Contents

About the Author

Ira Kalet was born on April 27, 1944 to Bernard "Ben" Kalet and Miriam "Millie" Pivnik in Stamford Connecticut where his father was managing the Kalet News Company. After Ben refused several extortion demands and the destruction of a delivery truck, the business was sold and the Kalet family moved to Long Island. Ira grew up in Rockville Centre with his sisters Gloria, Hazel, and his brother Stephen. His family were members of a conservative synagogue, Congregation Beth Israel in Hempstead, NY and he celebrated becoming a bar mitzvah in 1957.

He attended South Side High School and attended Cornell University where he majored in physics. After graduation he pursued graduate study at Princeton University obtaining a Ph.D. in theoretical physics in 1968. During his college years Ira became an enthusiastic hockey player, anti-war activist and violinist. He maintained these interests throughout his life.

He joined the faculty at the University of Washington, Physics Department in 1969. In the following year he taught at Sonoma State College in California, returning to Seattle in the summer of 1970 to become a mountain climber, teacher in alternative schools and prepare for admission to medical school. During that time, he met Terry Steele and they were married in 1973. In 1974 Ira and Terry moved to Philadelphia Pennsylvania where Ira taught at the University of Pennsylvania training secondary mathematics teachers and teaching physics at Upper Darby High School.

He decided not to complete a degree in medicine but returned to Seattle in 1978 when he was appointed to the faculty in the Department of Radiation Oncology. His most significant early work, in collaboration with Jon Jacky resulted in the development of a radiation therapy planning software (Plan32/Prism) that gained international recognition.

In 1993 Ira spent a year on sabbatical in Israel. He engaged in a collaborative research effort with Yoram Cohen, M.D. at the Ben Gurion Soroka Medical Center in Be'er Sheva Israel where he installed and trained staff in the use of Prism enabling patients to receive state-of-the art radiation therapy treatment in the northern Negev dessert.

He is especially known for his work on the application of artificial intelligence ideas to radiation therapy planning. From 1990 to 2004, Ira led the development of a new MS and PhD program at the UW creating the Biomedical and Health Informatics Program. In 2008 with the support of a publication grant from the National Library of Medicine, he published a book "Principles of Biomedical Informatics". The monography, the first ever of its kind, systematically developed the technical foundations of the young and merging academic discipline of biomedical informatics. His long term involvement in the field of biomedical informatics has been recognized by the NIH with a recent appointment to the National Library of Medicine Biomedical Library and Informatics Review Committee.

In 2005, Ira was appointed Director of Security and Networking for UW Medicine IT services. During the next few years, Ira reorganized the nacent Security Infrastructure Team into a strong networking group.

In his final years he received a grant from the National Library of Medicine to work on the Clinical Target Volume project which involved the use of artificial intelligence and modeling ideas to predict the local and regional spread of head and neck tumors. His co-PI Mark Whipple published a final paper after Ira's death in 2015.

After 32 years of service at the University of Washington he became Professor Emeritus in Radiation Oncology and Biomedical Informatics and maintained an active research agenda until a few weeks before his death in 2015.

He and his wife, Terry, joined Temple B'nai Torah (TBT), then located in Mercer Island, Washington, in 1989; along with their three children, Nathan, Alan and Brian. Ira was very active in Jewish education, teaching for about 9 years in the TBT Religious School. He also taught Adult Education classes on the prayer book, Torah and Talmud, served as a member and chair of the TBT Religious Practices Committee, and on the TBT Board of Directors. In 2000 they joined Congregation Beth Shalom in Seattle and maintained their membership in both communities.

Ira was also a very enthusiastic ice hockey player, serving as Captain of his team, the Hackers, in the Greater Seattle Hockey League.

This book contains Ira's stories about growing up in the sputnik era, a unique time in our nation's history where science was richly funded and exciting new ideas in physics were developing with Einstein, Feynman and others. Ira completed a draft of this manuscript only a few days before his death. It represents his thoughts about Torah from a unique perspective and the values and ethics he wanted to leave as a legacy.

Kalet News Company

Introduction

Temple B'nai Torah (TBT), our "Little Temple in the Woods" on Mercer Island, held regular Shabbat morning services, unusual for a Reform congregation in the 1990s. My wife, Terry, and I were among the small band of "regulars." Services at TBT involved a nice mix of Hebrew and English prayers, thoughtful commentaries from Rabbi James Mirel and inspiring singing of Cantor David Serkin-Poole. A bar or bat mitzvah of course would draw more of a crowd, adding a special flavor unique to the particular young person called to the Torah that day. Most of all, the friends we made among the congregants, the warm and wonderful families and children, made TBT a very special place. My writing journey begins with one such family.

The Negrin family, Michael, Robin and their daughter, Lorren, were not only ardent ice hockey fans, but also part owners of the Tacoma Rockets ice hockey team in the Western Hockey League. Terry and I had the great honor and pleasure to join them one evening at the Tacoma Dome for dinner and a game. The event was a little fund raiser for the Temple. So, on Saturday, December 13, 1997, the Shabbat morning that Lorren was called to the Torah as a bat mitzvah, I made sure to be there. One of the most wonderful parts of the service, added when there is a bar or bat mitzvah, is the presenting of gifts to the young person, most especially the gift of loving comments from his or her parents. This is of course in addition to the thoughtful commentary on the Torah portion, a D'var Torah, by the young person herself. Finally, one of the men of the congregation would come up and present a small gift on behalf of the Men's Club. Rabbi Mirel called on me that day to present the Men's Club gift to Lorren. I liked to make a comment or two relating the Torah portion to something I knew about the young person. I was teaching 7th grade at the TBT religious school and knew personally most, if not all, of the b'nai mitzvah.

The Torah portion that week, parashat Vayishlach, in Genesis, Chapter 32, tells the story of the reunion of Jacob and Esau after many years of estrangement. Verses 8-9 describe Jacob's anticipation, and plans for this event:

> "Jacob was greatly frightened; in his anxiety, he divided the people with him, and the flocks and herds and camels, into two camps, thinking, "If Esau comes to the one camp and attacks it, the other camp may yet escape."

Being an ice hockey fan myself, and a player from time to time, I explained to Lorren how similar this was to ice hockey, where the team has to spread out when skating down ice with the puck, so that if the opposition attacks the player with the puck he/she has the option to pass the puck across to a teammate, and in addition that takes advantage of the fact that the puck can be sent down the ice by passing, much faster than anyone can skate. My remarks were a bit lengthy. After I finished, as I stepped down from the Bimah, Rabbi Mirel quipped, "Thank you, Dr. Kalet, for your insightful comments. We are all looking forward to your forthcoming book, Torah, Ice Hockey and Astrophysics."

The author wearing a jersey from the Israeli hockey team 2015

I have taken somewhat longer than expected, but here, finally, is the book. I've broadened "Astrophysics" to include all of physics, and mathematics and computing as well. Not every chapter has something on all three topics, but you may find a connection of which I was not aware. Some chapters are transcripts of Torah commentaries (divrei Torah) that I was privileged to give at local synagogues in the Seattle area, along with some additional explanatory material. Some are accounts of thought-provoking experiences. Perhaps you will be inspired to write your own. There is much more to learn.

Enjoy!

Some Background on Jewish Tradition and History

The background information here should help explain what could otherwise be very obscure references to those unfamiliar with Jewish tradition, the Bible, other literary works, and the great sages and commentators on Judaism.

The Bible and the Oral Law

The Jewish tradition begins with the Torah, also known as The Five Books of Moses". The Hebrew text is handwritten on parchment sheets sewn together and rolled up as a scroll with two rollers. There are also printed versions, in standard book form, usually with a translation into English or other languages. These printed volumes also include commentaries and explanation, written or edited by modern scholars. The printed book version is known by the Hebrew, Chumash, from Chamesh, the Hebrew word for "five," referring to the five books.

It is an almost universal practice in the Jewish communities that a portion of the Torah is read aloud to the assembled community each week according to an annual or triennial schedule. The weekly readings follow the sequence of the written Torah, starting with Genesis 1:1 and ending a year later with the last verses of Deuteronomy. In the triennial schedule, about one third of each weekly portion is read the first year, the second third of each weekly portion is read in the second year, and in the third year the last third of each portion is read. So, no matter which schedule is followed, all the communities read from the same portion each week. This tradition is said to have been established by the Prophet Ezra, during the Babylonian Exile, around the 6th century BCE. The readings were (and still are) done during the morning service on the Sabbath (Shabbat), and also on Monday and Thursday mornings. These were times when the community would be assembled anyway, since Monday and Thursday were market days in ancient Babylon. The Monday and Thursday readings are short, just the first few paragraphs from the full weekly portion. The schedule of portions that is used today dates back to Maimonides, in the 12th century CE. The weekly portion is referred to as the "parashat hashavua," or "sidra" or sometimes just "parashah." Each weekly reading is further divided into smaller sections. Before each section is read, a member of the congregation or a guest is called to the reading platform (the "bimah"). This is a great honor, called an "aliyah" (meaning, "going up"), which involves reciting a blessing before and after the reading.

A custom rarely seen today is the use of a translator, along with the reader, to translate sentence by sentence from Hebrew to the vernacular (language of the community). A practice that is still very much in use today is to have an individual, not always a rabbi, provide an interpretation or commentary on some aspect of the parashah, often by assembling ideas or writings of the Sages, or others, and sometimes adding ideas of his or her own. This person is referred to as the Darshan, and the commentary is called a "D'var Torah" (a word of Torah). The second part of this book is a series of such commentaries (plural: "divrei Torah") that I had the privilege to give at local Seattle area synagogues on Shabbat mornings.

Some Sabbaths have special names, due to their significant places in the annual cycle of the Jewish calendar. The Sabbath between Rosh HaShanah and Yom Kippur is known as "Shabbat Shuvah," the Sabbath of Turning, since it is a time of reflection and return from the mistakes of the previous year to a life dedicated to Torah. The Sabbath before Pesach is known as "Shabbat HaGadol," the Great Sabbath, since it precedes the great holiday of Passover.

The complete Jewish Bible includes two additional sections, one of which is books attributed to the Prophets, and the other is the Writings, consisting of other literary works, attributed to various authors. The Writings include Psalms, Proverbs, Lamentations, The Song of Songs, Job, Esther, and others.

The Hebrew word for prophets is nevi'im, and "writings" translates as "ketuvim," so the Bible is usually referred to as "Tanach," an acronym for "Torah, Nevi'im, Ketuvim." So the Bible is essentially a small library of some of the greatest written works of Antiquity.

Our tradition says that Moses received two Torahs (teachings) on Mount Sinai, the Written Law, which is the Torah, and an Oral Law, which is to be passed down through the generations with each generation teaching it to the next. The Oral Law does not exist in written form, of course, but it is at least partly accessible through the Talmud, a compilation of the discussions, teachings, arguments and stories of the Sages from the time of the Roman occupation to about the 5th century C.E.

Greetings

When we visited Temple B'nai Torah the first time, Rabbi Mirel took time to introduce us to many others who were already members, and found some way to help us start a conversation. After we became members, which was not long after our first visit, he began to introduce visitors to me, mentioning something about me or the visitors that might be interesting and trigger a conversation. Sometime later, I decided that I should help out, without waiting to be introduced. Thus I learned how to do the mitzvah of welcoming visitors.

One Friday night, Rabbi Mirel devoted a sermon to this important topic. In his remarks he included a quote from the Talmud "It was related to R. Yochanan ben Zakkai that no man ever gave him greeting first, even a heathen in the street."

In January 2001 I was invited to (and attended) a reception to celebrate the opening of the Seattle Cancer Care Alliance (SCCA), a joint project of the University of Washington, the Fred Hutchinson Cancer Research Center and Seattle Children's Hospital, to provide unified and coordinated cancer care in our region. I helped set up the radiation oncology service and my radiation treatment planning software was in use there when they first started up. At the reception, I knew very few people, and after short visits with them, I didn't have anyone else to talk with. But I remembered Rabbi Mirel and Rabbi Yochanan, and noticed there was a young man who appeared to be alone, so I introduced myself and started a conversation. He was Jesse Fann, a Professor of Psychiatry whose clinical service was at the

SCCA. We talked about the challenges of cancer, about our families, Seattle, and the academic life.

Sometime later, during Passover in 2003, I was in the cancer ward at University of Washington Medical Center, in the second phase of treatment with Interleukin-2 infusion for my metastatic kidney cancer. This was one of the first of a great variety of treatments I've been through for metastases, and one of the most difficult. Interleukin-2 has the effect of stimulating one's immune system; giving very high doses of it can cause your immune system to activate to a level that recognizes and even in a few cases eliminates the cancer. However, it also causes horrible drops in blood pressure, huge fluid retention, and many other awful effects that must be managed by nurses who keep constant surveillance. The second phase was 10 days in the hospital. After about 5 days, I became very depressed and upset, not because of the difficulty of the treatment, but because of the gripping fear that after going through all this horror, it might not work. My nurse brought in the psychiatry resident, a very nice young woman, who listened at length to my anxiety that I might not live long enough to take care of my family and do the things I had hoped to do. After some time, she explained that she would be back in a few minutes with the Psychiatry Attending Physician, who would also see me. This is the routine, the Resident sees you first, then the Attending, who is a faculty member. And in walked Jesse Fann.

Above: Jesse Fann

Twists and Turns

Ira and his parents at graduation from South Side High School

For many parents, one of the most puzzling and complex decision processes their children faced is that of choosing a college or university to attend after high school. When I was a teenager, there were several encyclopedic books that provided current information about thousands of colleges. The colleges themselves were happy to send catalogs and other information to prospective students. School guidance counselors were an official resource, though not always able to speak from recent experience. In my case, however, it was largely by accident.

My friend Jim Ritter was very interested in attending Princeton University, and had heard of a program offered by some colleges called "Early Decision." In this program, you, the high school student, applied, by a very early deadline, only to your top choice college. The college reviewed all these early applications and made admissions offers to the top students. By applying to the Early Decision program, you agreed to accept an admission offer to your top choice school if admitted. The advantage was that at that point you are all set, and are spared the agony of waiting to hear from all the schools, and then decide among them. If you did not get admitted through Early Decision, you could still be considered in the regular pool, and could then also apply to other colleges. I waited in line at the school counseling office after school one day with Jim, because we hung out together a lot anyway and I was curious to see how it would turn out for him.

The guidance counselor sadly explained to Jim that Princeton did not have an Early Decision program, and without hesitating, turned to me, thinking I was also in line for information. She queried, "So, Ira, what college are you interested in?" I was caught totally off guard, and had no idea where I wanted to go, but had heard of other Ivy League schools, and for no apparent reason, said, "Um, well, Cornell." Her enthusiastic response carried the day. "Ira, you are in luck. Cornell is offering Early Decision for the first time this year. Here are the forms, and here is what you need to do…" Before I could catch my breath, I was already tied up in the application process.

I then read the Cornell catalogs in the school library and looked up Cornell in some other references. It looked great. What did I know? So, I did the application, and went home to tell my parents. They were apprehensive. I come from a family that struggled through the Great Depression, and my father was minimally employed as was my mother. They said it would be a lot less expensive to go to a more local school like the Polytechnic Institute of Brooklyn, so I could live at home and commute. My parents could so well read the expression on my face, I didn't have to say much. They reassured me that if I worked summers and got scholarships we would manage somehow with Cornell. And we did.

Cornell

After I was admitted to Cornell, my parents took me there for a few days to get acquainted with the campus and its people (yes, later to become "my people"). The campus sprawls over a large hilltop above the City of Ithaca, New York, and above Lake Cayuga, 38 miles long, the longest of the five "Finger Lakes" of upstate New York. Although New York City was well known throughout the world, the rest of New York State was (and likely still is) unfamiliar to most. It is very rural, with large forests and old mountains, not high even by Washington Cascades standards, but prominent and largely uninhabited. Much of upper New York State is actually a state park, Adirondack Park. This park is the largest state park in the, U.S., and also is larger than any of the U.S. national parks in the "lower 48" states.

The University was founded by Ezra Cornell and Andrew Dickson White in 1865, as a New York State Land Grant institution as well as a privately endowed institution. Ezra Cornell's motto, "I would found an institution where any person can find instruction in any study" is on the University's official seal.

The diversity of organizational units and fields of study were unparalleled at the time. By the 1960s, the Cornell Mathematics and Physics departments had achieved the highest status and recognition in those fields. It was thrilling to read of all the different course offerings, and to see who was teaching them.

I confess to being a little intimidated too, but I got over it. Aside from the spectacular physical beauty, I enjoyed the exposure to students studying agriculture, home economics, industrial and labor relations, hotel administration, and of course the usual collection of traditional Arts and Sciences.

Cornell's Engineering College had a quadrangle that radically departed from the traditional "College Gothic" style. The Engineering buildings looked like giant toy boxes, with huge uniformly colored panels, each color corresponding to a different department. The Mathematics department was a more standard "College Gothic", located on the Arts quadrangle (the "Quad" for short). Just walking from one class to another or to the libraries was a significant exercise. In the Spring and Fall it was a walk through a visual paradise. In the Winter, it got so cold, there was ice (or snow) on the walkways all winter. Despite having layers of real winter coats and warm clothing underneath, we often had to stop and enter an intermediate building between our starting point and destination, in order to thaw out.

The College of Agriculture maintained a working dairy which supplied milk, cream, butter and eggs to the campus food services. There was also a Veterinary College, and large animal facilities. In addition to the usual intercollegiate sports, Cornell had a polo barn for indoor polo. I went to one of these polo matches, and it was terrifying to see these huge horses running in such a confined space making tight maneuvers as demanded by their riders. A good experience to have once.

More exciting than the polo barn was Lynah Rink, a beautiful ice rink with seating for spectators to come to Cornell varsity intercollegiate ice hockey games (Eastern College Athletic Conference, or ECAC, not Ivy League). But better than watching, the rink had public skating sessions, and a "learn to play ice hockey program" through the Intramural Sports division. I had been on ice skates twice before that but I signed up, bought some basic equipment, and the Intramural program provided the rest. I was a math and science geek but no one seemed to mind.

Cornell Scramblers

In the Spring, I enrolled in a German literature class, a real struggle for me. I had no patience to do translation on my own, and insufficient knowledge of vocabulary and grammar to read fluently. However, I was reading an assignment, Johann Wolfgang von Goethe's "Novelle," chapter 1, while sitting at the top of Library Slope on a beautiful Spring day, and came upon the following sentence: "hierauf nun steht gemauert ein Turm, doch niemand wu¨ßte zu sagen, wo die Natur aufh¨ort, Kunst und Handwerk aber anfangen." It was the first sentence I could translate without consulting my German-English dictionary. "Ahead, a man-made tower stood, but one could not really say where Nature left off, where art and craft began." And as I lifted my head from the book, looking down the vast grassy expanse of Library Slope, past the trees, the old Cornell men's dormitories came into view, a chain of classic college gothic style stone structures: McFadden Hall, Lyon Hall, a covered walkway, and finally, Baker Tower.

The Baker dormitories were built in 1928 and the years following. I lived there twice during my undergraduate years, once in Baker Tower, and once in Lyon Hall. The rooms are well insulated (the buildings are thick stone) and well heated, providing a refuge through the cold and snowy Ithaca winters. In those days, the rooms did not have private telephones, and cellular telephones did not exist. There were only shared wall telephones in the hallways. So we got to know our dormitory neighbors by answering the telephones, as well as just through normal proximity. Classmates lived nearby, and we often worked together on homework assignments. Physics and mathematics being somewhat esoteric subjects, we also shared a lot of "in" jokes which would make no sense if you did not understand physics. One friend, Max Mintz, was studying electrical engineering, and shared a lot of classes because of the overlap of this area with physics. So we all knew Maxwell's Equations, the four basic laws of classical electricity and magnetism. Partly from the name, and partly out of admiration for the beauty, symmetry and universality of these equations, Max often insisted that any problem could be solved using them. So one day I suggested to Max that we had a physical problem here in the dormitory that could not be solved by Maxwell's equations. It was the fact that the telephone in the hallway rang at all hours and woke people from their much needed rest. He responded, "Of course this can be solved by Maxwell's equations. I will show you." He took a piece of paper, wrote the equations on it, took a screwdriver and opened the telephone box. Then he crumpled the paper, stuffed it between the clapper and the bell, and indeed our problem was solved.

Above: The main residence building, Ms Kalbfeisch's home, served as our quarters. It was really comfortable; I enjoyed many evenings reading Plato's dialogues in the living room when I needed a break from radio astronomy.

August Kalbfleisch

Summers for college students have always been challenging times. Most of us needed to earn some money toward the cost of the following year's education and living expenses. It was certainly possible to find a job in the commercial world, doing relatively mundane tasks for a minimum wage, but there were also a few opportunities, especially for science and engineering students, to actually learn on the job, a kind of science apprenticeship, or Summer Scholarship. Of these, the most exciting were the ones that involved participation in research projects. I had the good fortune to participate two summers in one such program.

Somehow I learned of a program run by the American Museum of Natural History Hayden Planetarium, supported by a grant from the National Science Foundation. It had been made possible by a gift to the Museum from August Kalbfleisch in her will. She owned a 94-acre plot of land in Dix Hills, Long Island, near Huntington. This land was relatively undeveloped and had large tracts of woods, open fields, a large main residence, a carriage house with rooms upstairs, originally probably a resident caretaker's quarters, and a single family home at the entrance gate. The Museum established the Kalbfleisch estate as a field research station, where Museum staff could conduct field studies. Dr. Wesley Lanyon, a curator in the Ornithology Department of the Museum, served as the resident director, and lived in the home at the entrance with his family. In addition, the site hosted a radio astronomy project, directed by Dr. Kenneth L. Franklin, of the Hayden Planetarium. and several field biology projects run by Museum staff. Each Summer between 9 and 12 students were selected from among a pool of applicants, to participate in the various projects. I was selected to work on the radio astronomy project for the Summers of 1962 and 1963.

We students lived in the main estate building, which had an ample dining room, living room and study downstairs, and several small and large sleeping quarters upstairs. The largest rooms were arranged as dormitories, and a few students had private quarters, in particular the one female student participant each of the two summers I was there. A full time housekeeper came in each day to cook our meals, and take care of other house chores. We helped the housekeeper, but there were no assigned tasks; it was done on an informal basis, almost like and extended family.

Dr. Lanyon had two students who worked on bird banding, field observation and other ornithology projects. One evening he did a taxidermy demonstration, which at first was jarring, but at the end, the specimen was so perfectly preserved, it was really amazing. Other projects involved plant biology and ecology, study of small mammals in their natural habitats, and herpetology projects.

Above: The site maintenance man, Bill Hutchins and his young assistant, Geoff Kauffman.

The labs were in the carriage house, a few hundred feet up the driveway from the residence. When you went in up the stairs, the botany and mammalogy/ herpetology labs were on the left, and the radio astronomy lab was to the right. In 1955, while at the Carnegie Institution of Washington, Dr. Franklin and Bernard Burke discovered surprisingly strong radio emissions that they determined were coming from the planet Jupiter. The frequency range of these radio noise bursts are in the 15-meter amateur radio band, so are detectable with relatively inexpensive equipment. Dr. Franklin had set up two antennas at the Kalbfleisch property, about 690 feet apart. They were connected back to the radio astronomy laboratory, which occupied most of the upstairs area of the garage. The rest of the garage housed space for the other students and their projects. I was one of two students working on the radio telescope. I knew a lot about electronic equipment (I was a licensed amateur radio operator back then) but had only rudimentary knowledge of astronomy.

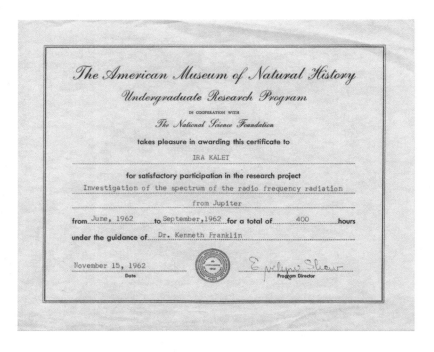

That was fine, because the radio telescope electronics had lots of room for improvement. The two antennas functioned as an "interferometer," so that as an object moved through the sky, the time it took radio signals to reach one antenna relative to the other would shift. This slight difference can be detected by an electronic circuit called a "phase switch." The two signals are alternately added and subtracted to each other under control of an audio signal. The audio signal would thus be imposed on the combined radio signal, and it in turn would change its phase relative to the original audio oscillator so that you would get a wave-like output as the source of the radio noise moved across the sky. The magnitude of the wave produced by the interferometer is proportional to the intensity of the radio signals coming to the antennas.

Dr. Franklin came out to the site usually once a week, to discuss our progress, help with anything we might need, and provide encouragement and instruction. We looked forward to these visits, and decided in anticipation of one of them to properly dress up the Tektronix oscilloscope that was one of our main test instruments. We ourselves were not so tidy.

Dr. Franklin

Dr. Kenneth Franklin, makes notations on a radiation recording at the Kalbfleisch Field Research Station in Dix Hills.

JUPITER CALLING!

★ ★ ★   ★ ★ ★

Radio Waves Register at LI Lab

An experiment in radio astronomy being conducted in Dix Hills may someday unlock the secrets of the planet Jupiter.

In 1955 astronomers discovered the largest planet in our solar system, Jupiter, gives off radiation that can be detected by shortwave radio.

Dr. Kenneth Franklin of the American Museum of Natural History and Hayden Planetarium has for years headed a project at the Kalbfleisch Field Research Station off Deer Park Avenue, Dix Hills, to learn more about this radiation.

The research station, the former estate of Augusta Kalbfleisch who died in 1956, is not limited to this one experiment.

Dr. Wesley E. Lanyon, the station's resident director, has supervised experiments with radar devices adapted to test the flight-speed of birds and projects involving the natural cycles of plants and their relation to animals, among other things.

Dr. Franklin's attempts at measuring the radio waves from Jupiter, however, are receiving more public attention than anything else now going on at the 94-acre estate.

LAST SUMMER two college students assisted Dr. Franklin with the delicate and difficult work.

One of them, Ira Kalet, 19, of 300 Willow St., South Hempstead, is a junior majoring in physics at Cornell University.

He received a National Science Foundation award which enabled him to work at the Dix Hills station. Next he'd like to work at Brookhaven National Laboratories.

Interested in physics since he was a child, he helped to mount and directionalize the all-important antenna which helps detect Jupiter's radio waves.

Kalet also did some theoretical research so complicated that even Dr. Franklin said it will take him a while to understand it.

What produces the emissions that come from Jupiter? Why do they occur when they do? What causes the waves to come in intermittent bursts?

No one yet has the answers to those questions.

★ ★ ★

AT THE MOMENT the project at Kalbfleisch is still in its early stages, transferring the impulses received by its radio on 26 megacycles—that seems to be Jupiter's wave length — to paper by means of a pen held in a mechanical arm activated by the radio "bursts."

Dr. Franklin, who lived in Glen Cove for five years before moving to New Jersey last June, spends only one day a week at the research facilities at this time of year.

He studies the data gathered by his "writing radio" and then returns to work on other things in his Manhattan office during the remaining part of the week.

At the moment, he said, he has no idea where his current experiments will lead.

Just as last year he hadn't planned to forsake Long Island for his new home.

"I decided suddenly," he said, " I was spending too much time traveling."

Even scientists dealing with planets millions of light years away from earth can become frustrated by the Long Island Expressway.

The antennas were a pretty well known design, a 3-element Yagi-Uda array in which only the central element connected to the receiver, acting as a sort of dipole. The other elements absorbed and retransmitted signals, so they enhanced the sensitivity. I found a way to derive a formula from some handbooks and my knowledge of Maxwell's Equations, so that we could account for the variations in sensitivity in the different directions. Fortunately, there were two other radio sources in this same (15-meter Ham Radio) band, called Cygnus A and Cassiopeia A (because of their visual location in those two constellations). Their relative signal strength was measured by others and was well known. We were able to use measurements of these two known sources to check the accuracy of our formula. The formula predictions were within about 3% of the known values. This project confirmed that, as Max Mintz had observed earlier in the dormitories, any problem could be solved using Maxwell's equations, even ones for which they were appropriate!

For the enjoyment of those who have some exposure to mathematics and physics, Gauss's Law states that electric charges generate electric fields, and the charges are conserved (neither created nor destroyed). Faraday's Law states that a changing magnetic field creates an electric field even if there are no charges present. The third equation, needed for completeness, asserts that there are no magnetic charges. The final equation combines two ideas, electric currents (moving charges) create magnetic fields, and that a changing electric field also creates a magnetic field. These four equations indeed account in at least a partial way for most of the technology of our modern world. The intricacy of solving the equations and applying them to different devices and circumstances is an adventure like climbing the highest mountains. It takes you to a remote and remarkable world. Unfortunately, you cannot experience this world unless you are willing to learn mathematics. But some do, just as there are numbers of people who climb mountains and pay the entry price by learning the techniques, and training for that adventure.

Princeton

The decision to go to Princeton University for graduate study in theoretical physics was definitely not an accident. I was interested in learning about the foundations of quantum field theory (Wightman) and about General Relativity and gravity (Wheeler). Princeton was the only place that seemed to have both.

I spent my first year as a theoretical physics graduate student at Princeton with Prof. John Wheeler, then graduate student Kip Thorne (who was just finishing), and many other people involved in gravity theory, and the beginnings of exploration of a quantum theory of gravity. I was learning about spin manifolds. I knew about the Lie groups O (3) and SU (2) but not their relationship. At Wheeler's suggestion, I went to John Milnor for help. He was then a young faculty member in the Princeton Math Department. Of course his office in Fine Hall was just down the corridor and around the corner from the theory wing of Palmer Lab. Prof. Milnor very kindly explained about rotations and paths through the rotation group by taking off his belt, handing me the buckle end, and showing how the belt could represent equivalence classes of paths through the rotation group, with his end representing an arbitrary element of the group and my end representing the identity element. It became clear from manipulating the belt that a 360-degree rotation did not belong to the same equivalence class as the identity, but 720 did. And the most amazing thing of all was that his pants did not fall down.

The author in his chemistry lab located in the basement of his home on Hempstead Ave. He would purchase chemicals in Manhattan and take the train home to mix them together. After one mistake the basement was filling with possible toxic fumes so he went upstairs and told his mother not to go into the basement for a while. She said sure and that was that.

The decade of the 1950s vibrated with enthusiasm for science, mathematics, engineering and technology throughout the Western World. One of the enormous differences between World War II and previous wars was that technology and its scientific underpinnings played a critical role. The most visible and dramatic sign was the development and use of the Atomic Bomb.

Less obvious but probably far more important was the development of radar and its use not only in navigation but in detecting and targeting enemy airplanes. The extensive use of air warfare was itself a significant change from previous wars. The development of encryption and decryption, secret codes and the use of that brand new invention, the digital computer, also generated interest in science, mathematics and technology. This was the beginning of a large (and for some two decades, sustained) investment by the United States government and many others in basic scientific research and in science and mathematics education. Because the atomic bomb, and later (1952) the hydrogen bomb, had come very clearly from the basic and fundamental research of the first half of the century, it was widely accepted that supporting basic research was very important. There were many opportunities for pursuing explorations solely out of interest in deepening our understanding without knowing or even speculating on what the commercial payoff or benefit to society might be. In 1957, the first Earth satellite went into orbit. I remember vividly my friends and I searching the night sky for this tiny blip. That year also was the beginning of the International Geophysical Year, an 18-month long collaboration among 67 countries, including the then Union of Soviet Socialist Republics (USSR). Projects investigated cosmic rays, solar flares, seismology, gravity, oceanography and other earth sciences.

My interest and involvement in science began at a young age. By fifth grade, I knew about electric circuits, electromagnets, and a variety of other things. One day my fifth grade teacher decided that she needed a bell or buzzer to get the attention of the class, at times when we might be reading or working on our own. She asked me and one of my classmates to put together a box with a battery, buzzer, and button, for this purpose. My classmate didn't know anything about electricity but was very skilled with his hands, so I figured out how everything should be connected, and he mounted all the parts in the box and secured the wires. It worked well and was a fun collaboration of "brains and brawn". Many years later I came across a more elaborate box, containing a switch. When you toggled the switch, the lid would open and an artificial hand would come out, that turned off the switch, went back into the box and the lid would then close.

It was fun and thought provoking. When I taught in the UW Biomedical and Health Informatics program I used this as an example of a self-regulating system and wrote a small computer program that simulated the box and its sequence of operations. Later I discovered that another researcher had written a computer program to simulate the cycle that living cells follow as they grow and prepare for mitosis. The cell is stimulated by an outside influence, turning on some gene activity. The genes activate and deactivate each other in a fairly complex pattern, and after a short time, the entire set of genes turns off and becomes quiescent again. These programs are described in detail in my book,

"Principles of Biomedical Informatics." So, my explorations and tinkering as a child led logically to my later career in biomedical computing.

A self-regulating box, that turns itself off when you try to turn it on.
Photo courtesy of Hanns-Martin Wagner, http://www.kugelbahn.ch/)

For a young student with a talent for math and science and a passionate interest in both, the post-war era of the 1950s was a Golden Age. Being in the New York City area, our schools organized field trips to Brookhaven National Laboratory, where the largest particle accelerators in the world were being built or already operating. Mr. Wizard (Don Herbert) entertained us on television with wondrous and fun demonstrations of principles of physics and chemistry. There was even an early morning television program and accompanying text and workbook to help young people learn Russian, which was not yet taught in any schools.

Like many other kids in my neighborhood, I loved baseball, played stickball in our driveway, and at the school yard, and saved up my *Elsie the Cow* ice cream wrappers, ten of which would get a general admission ticket to a Brooklyn Dodgers game for only 75 cents. My brother and I had hundreds of baseball cards, many of which would be worth serious amounts of money today. We clipped them to our bicycle front forks with clothespins and loved the flapping sound they made as we pedaled through the neighborhood. I sometimes wonder if Mickey Mantle or Jackie Robinson or Willie Mays ever thought about the fact that each day thousands of cardboard copies of their smiling faces were rapping against the spokes of bicycles of all sizes.

But more than baseball, or the beaches in the Summer, or snowball fights and snow sculptures in the Winter, I spent most of my time in the public school libraries, and the Rockville Centre public library, reading every serious mathematics or physics book I could find. In Hempstead, the next town to the North, there was a small bookstore, called Womrath's. That also became a hangout for me. I saved my earnings from my newspaper route, and began a small library of my own. One day I heard about a fabulous book store in the City (yes, growing up on Long Island, we knew there was only one real city, New York, actually Manhattan). This book store had college texts, and it published a series of wonderfully concise paperback books under its own name, the Barnes and Noble College Outline Series. I saved enough money for a trip on my own into the City, two bus rides to Jamaica, in Queens, and a long subway ride from there to midtown Manhattan. It took about an hour and a half each way, but I had the whole day. Arriving at the original Barnes and Noble, I was confronted by six floors of books, on every subject imaginable. An entire floor was occupied by science and mathematics. I was in Paradise, the Garden of Eden, and nothing was forbidden.

Most every Sunday afternoon, my family drove to Flushing, in Queens, where my grandparents on my father's side lived. It was a regular family gathering, with my father's siblings and their spouses and children, my cousins. My grandfather was in the newspaper distribution business, not just newspapers, but magazines and other print media, but most important to us kids, comic books. He usually brought home two bundles of comics with the title banners cut off. The collection usually included the entire range of popular comics of the time, Superman, Captain Marvel, Wonder Woman, Archie, Mickey Mouse, Donald Duck, and on and on. But for me there was another attraction to these Sunday excursions. My Uncle Eugene is an electronics engineer, now retired.

Irving, Eugene and Donald Kalet

Back then, he had accumulated a collection of electronic tests instruments, which he used in his studies, but which he no longer needed professionally. He showed me how they worked and I was allowed to connect them together to experiment and learn for myself. There was an audio signal generator, an oscilloscope, a multimeter for measuring voltages, currents and resistance, and other instruments, of which I no longer recall the details. The audio signal generator had two adjustable outputs, so I could connect one to the oscilloscope X input, and the other to the Y input. Changing the frequencies, amplitudes and phases of the two signals would produce unlimited varieties of Lissajous figures, the patterns that help us understand harmonic motion. Getting the frequencies just right would make the patterns stationary, otherwise they would vibrate or rotate or move around in other ways. Uncle Eugene was a very patient teacher and appreciated how much fun I had with these very expensive and professional toys.

A few of my friends, too, had this passion for science and math, and books. We learned about things in mathematics which were never taught in the schools, the theory of groups, topology, curved space (Riemannian and Lobachevskian geometry), calculus, and much more. By the time our high school started teaching calculus (the 1959-1960 school year) my friends and I were already learning it on our own. Someone discovered a little book by Sylvanus P. Thompson, titled, "Calculus Made Easy," first published in 1910 and still available today. The book begins with what Thompson called an ancient Simian proverb, "What one fool can do, another can." We understood he was reassuring us that what followed would be achievable, even by fools like us. The following year, 1960-61, our Senior year, we were very fortunate to have a wonderful teacher for calculus, Alice Reeve. Ms. Reeve knew her stuff and it was a great treat for us finally to have someone teach us who knew more math than we did.

Ninth grade student working out algebraic computation.

These boys are applying their knowledge of mathematics to mechanical drawing problems.

In 1958, my friends and I began meeting regularly to discuss the possibility of building a cyclotron at our high school. The cyclotron was invented in the 1930s by Ernest Lawrence, a physicist at the University of California, Berkeley. It uses a large electromagnet with a disk-shaped vacuum chamber between the North and South poles of the electromagnet. Protons (Hydrogen ions) are introduced in the center, and are made to go in spiral paths until they are at the outer edge of the chamber. Then they are deflected out and made to collide with various targets to study the structure of atomic nuclei. The protons travel inside two D shaped half-disks facing each other.

One is given a very high negative voltage, while the other gets a very high positive voltage. Protons, being positive, are attracted to the negative half-disk (called a "Dee") and repelled by the positive one. Once inside the Dee, they coast but follow a semicircular path, to again return to the gap between the Dees. At this point, you switch the polarity so the positive Dee is now negative and the negative one is positive. The proton is then pushed (pulled) across the gap into the other Dee, where it again circles around. Each time it crosses the gap, it gains energy and so goes in a larger semicircle, until, reaching the periphery, it is deflected out through a small window. The voltage has to change very rapidly, at about the rate of a short-wave radio signal, so one can use a modified version of a short-wave radio transmitter to provide the voltage, and power, to drive the protons around. Lawrence's great discovery was that the laws of physics work out so that the protons take the same amount of time around, regardless of whether they are in small semicircles or larger ones. The protons in the larger circles are moving faster, which just balances the increased distance. The magnet strength needed also turns out to be the same for all such semicircles, so it is feasible to build a magnet with a constant strength in the area of the chamber, and a constant frequency radio transmitter. This is the cyclotron principle.

While the principle is simple, in practice you need a lot of machinery, vacuum pumps and gauges, powerful radio transmitters, thick concrete shielding, and elaborate apparatus to do experiments with the high energy protons. The shielding can be concrete walls as much as 15 feet thick. The power required to get the needed magnet strength and run the transmitters can be as much as would be used by a small town. The transmitters that provide the voltage are as powerful as those used by commercial radio stations. So these "atom smashers" are expensive and take up significant space. This led to a series of cartoons, "The Cyclotron as Seen By..." which may be found at the web site of the American Institute of Physics,

Of course, there are some complications that require the actual machine to have some modifications of this very simple idea, but that all got worked out, and many cyclotrons were built around the world. One such is in the

Radiation Oncology department of the University of Washington, where I worked for many years. This machine was built in the early 1980s. The proton beam coming out of the cyclotron is directed on a small slug of Beryllium, which generates a neutron beam through a nuclear reaction. We then use the neutron beam to treat cancers. For some kinds of tumors, neutrons are relatively more effective than the other more conventional forms of radiation therapy. Only a few such facilities are operating through-out the world. I helped build the University of Washington cyclotron and neutron therapy facility. It is the most advanced and sophisticated facility of its kind, and I believe it has saved many lives over the last 30 years.

Our little high school group began writing to various sources for help, and we got some remarkable responses. From United States Steel Corporation, who we just asked about steel prices and cost of fabrication, I got a telephone call at home one day. The official who called said that US Steel would like to donate the steel for our cyclotron project. Of course, it had not been approved yet by the school administration but we were thrilled at their interest.

My Uncle Eugene again played a role, in which he provided for us a design for a very high powered oscillator circuit we could build. This oscil-lator would provide the voltage for the Dees of the cyclotron.

We also wrote to the Physics Department at Brookhaven National Laboratory with some questions. We got a response, which is reproduced here. Included with the letter were reprints of two articles, one from Scientific American, about a group like ours at El Cerrito High School in California, who earlier had indeed successfully built a small cyclotron. One of the questions we asked in my letter was what process or permissions or licensing we might need in order to do the project and use the cyclotron after it was working. As you can see in the letter, the reply assured us, "no government licensing is required to operate a cyclotron." That was 1959. Rest assured, Dear Reader, that the situation is very different today, and there are a great many regulations that have to be followed.

We all graduated without ever beginning to build our cyclotron, but we learned a great deal from attempting to write convincing plans. We continued to read about mathematics and physics, particularly "modern" physics, the quantum theory, Einstein's special and general theories of relativity, and gravity. We learned about anti-matter. For every elementary particle, it seems, there is a corresponding anti-particle. The anti-particles could in principle make up "anti-atoms" and in a larger sense, anti-matter. An anti-particle has the same mass as its corresponding ordinary particle, and the same intrinsic angular momentum, or spin (some of the particles behave as if they are spinning like a top). If the particle has an electric charge, the anti-particle has the opposite charge. So an anti-proton would have the same mass (about 1800 times the mass of an electron) and 1/2 unit of spin, but would be negatively charged. The anti-electron, which would be positively charged, had actually been observed and was named "positron." Photons are their own anti-particles. When particles and anti-particles collide, they are annihilated and their energy is converted into photons or other forms of energy. To us it seemed that the force of gravity was separate and different from the electromagnetic force. Gravity (for ordinary matter) is always attractive, and objects pull each other together.

BROOKHAVEN NATIONAL LABORATORY
ASSOCIATED UNIVERSITIES, INC.
UPTON. L. I. N.Y.
TEL. YAPHANK 4·6262   REFER:

DEPARTMENT OF
PHYSICS

28 July 1961

Mr. Ira Kalet
300 Willow Street
South Hempstead, New York

Dear Mr. Kalet:

The experiment you ask about in your letter is indeed of great importance. Its execution is, however, so tremendously difficult, that so far no one has dared to consider it seriously. Let me correct myself, the effect of gravity on a beam of slow neutrons was observed and measured here at Brookhaven. The results were just what one expected. A reprint is enclosed.

For a beam of charged particles the problem of observing the gravitational attraction seems beyond our present techniques. In order to focus the beam which, as you suggest yourself, is necessary, one must use magnetic and electric fields whose force on the particle is billions times larger than the weak gravitational forces. A gravitational change in the plane of their path will thus be completely obscured by immeasurable small uncertainties in the magnetic field which keeps the particles focused.

The problem is especially important for antiparticles. Could these antiparticles experience a gravitational repulsion instead of attraction? Unfortunately at present the small number of antiparticles produced with high energy accelerators and their short existence before annihilation makes answering this question another billion times more difficult. However, I am convinced that the answer will be found eventually. Some indirect method of measurement combined with some brilliant new ideas are needed to make progress along those lines. Perhaps some young physicist next week or a hundred years from now will come up with the answer.

Don't be discouraged by this letter. If you continue to study

Mr. Kalet   - 2 -   28 July 1961

physics you may come up with questions which may be less important
but easier to answer. And, if you are lucky and really good, you
might even find the answers to moderately important problems. There
are many still to be solved.

If you and your colleague want to see some of the physics research
at Brookhaven, let me know, perhaps we can arrange an afternoon for
such a visit.

Sincerely,

S. A. Goudsmit

SAG:poh

We wondered if anti-matter would be attracted to ordinary matter, or perhaps repelled, giving rise to anti-gravity. We did not know how to answer this question from what we already knew, so again we wrote to Brookhaven National Laboratory, to the Physics Department. This time we got a reply from Dr. Samuel Goudsmit, the Physics Department chair and a very famous physicist, one of the people who thought up the idea that particles spin like tops. He wrote that to measure anti-particles under the influence of gravity alone was well beyond the capability of any physics laboratory in existence or even imaginable at that time. He did say that at Brookhaven a group had measured the effect of gravity on neutrons, which was much easier since they are not affected much by electric or magnetic fields, even the Earth's magnetic field. The result was that the neutrons are pulled towards the Earth like everything else we know, at exactly the same rate of acceleration. His letter invited us to come to visit Brookhaven sometime when everything was operating (we had already been to the annual Visitor's Day, when everything is shut down and you don't really get to see all that much). We were very thrilled. My friend Jim Ritter and I drove in his Mom's Renault Dauphine, tinier even than the Volkswagen Bug. The guards at the Laboratory entrance were expecting us and directed us to the Physics Department, where we found Dr. Goudsmit's office. He had arranged a full itinerary.

One of the most impressive facilities we saw was the giant alternating gradient synchrotron, or AGS, the largest "atom smasher" in the world at the time, while it was in operation. It was a huge donut shaped ring in a circular tunnel about one half mile around. Roughly once a second, a bunch of protons would be accelerated around the ring until they reached unimaginable energy, and close to the speed of light. The beam of protons then could be sent into an 80-inch-long tank of liquid Hydrogen, cooled to a few degrees above absolute zero.

The injection of the protons into the ring would make a ping sound that could be heard almost anywhere on the laboratory grounds. Just before that the liquid hydrogen would be compressed by an enormous piston, and then released so it was superheated. The protons (and any other particles) passing through would leave trails of bubbles where they caused the liquid hydrogen to boil. So, as we stood there in this awesome building with the bubble chamber (as it was called), every second we would alternately hear a loud thump of the piston, and then a soft ping from the proton beam. THUMP-ping THUMP-ping it was like nothing else on Earth.

At Cornell University, where I went as an undergraduate, the Newman Laboratory of Nuclear Studies was the home of a smaller synchrotron, that produced a powerful beam of electrons instead of protons. This was useful, too, for different kinds of experiments. My junior year at Cornell, as part of my financial aid (work-study) I was hired as a night operator for the Cornell synchrotron. The job itself was boring, but the opportunity to meet famous physicists and participate in their work was thrilling.

In the Summer of 1964, between my junior year and senior year in college, I got to spend the Summer at Brookhaven in their undergraduate research program. I struggled to write computer programs that would automatically scan bubble chamber pictures to detect the bubble trails of the particles and calculate their properties. That was how I learned that image processing and pattern recognition were not good career choices for me. Humans did a much better job of scanning the films. At each pulse of the beam through the chamber, three cameras would snap photos of the bubble trails. A typical experiment would involve several million pictures and would take a few days of running time. A crew of women worked there in the laboratory scanning through the developed film after the experimental run, looking for interesting patterns and then tracing the tracks with a digitizing machine. Sometimes out of a million pictures, only a few would have the track patterns the physicists were looking for, as the interesting events were very rare.

Throughout, I devoured any reading matter I could find about elementary particles, not just the proton, neutron and electron, which built up atoms, but the new discoveries, mesons, neutrinos, the so-called strange particles, and the new ideas of how the mathematical Theory of Groups could organize these families and even predict new ones, yet to be discovered in the millions of bubble chamber pictures generated at Brookhaven, and at CERN, the European Centre for Nuclear Research, where another large synchrotron was operating, similar to the AGS at Brookhaven. The idea that these particles could be explained as combinations of more elementary entities called "quarks" also was developed then.

Above: The author at the operator's console of the Cornell University Electron Synchrotron, at Newman Laboratory of Nuclear Studies

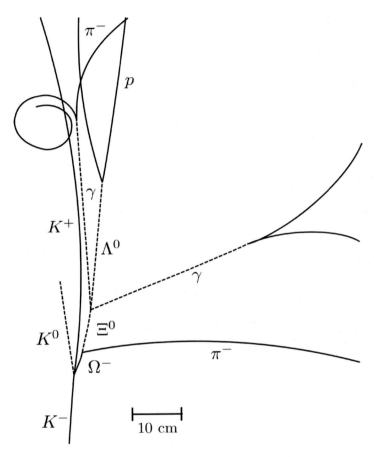

A schematic diagram of the bubble chamber picture tracks. The original was produced at Brookhaven National Laboratory and is the public domain.

The quark theory, also colloquially called, "The Eightfold Way," is most often credited to Murray Gell-Mann of California Institute of Technology and Yuval Ne'eman, of Tel Aviv University. One of the predictions of this theory was that a heavy particle, named the Omega minus ($\Omega-$), should show up in collisions of K−mesons with protons in a bubble chamber. In 1964, three pictures from Brookhaven (out of a run of a million or so) showed short tracks that were confirmed to be the Omega minus. An article in Physical Review Letters, volume 12, number 8, February 24, 1964, by

V.E. Barnes et. al., reports this startling discovery. To my friends and I, this was one of the most exciting events in our lifetimes, more significant than the satellites and the later landing of a person on the Moon. It was even better than the Brooklyn Dodgers winning the 1955 Baseball World Series.

In the decades following the discovery of the Omega minus ($\Omega-$) particle, a more developed mathematical model emerged, identifying which of the many particles were fundamental and which were related to the fundamental particles, in more complex combinations. This model, called "The Standard Model" became gradually more accepted as its consequences were understood.

However, things were not quite right. The Standard Model is an example of a general type of mathematical system called a "Quantum Field Theory." The basic principles of a Quantum Field Theory include very abstract mathematics, in which the elementary particles are represented as infinite dimensional vectors, which obey symmetry principles from which one can infer other properties, and discover relationships and phenomena that are not at all obvious by just looking at the basic mathematics. One example of this is the phenomenon called a "black hole." That such objects might exist was known only after solving Einstein's gravitational field equations in different situations, and how those solutions look different as you change the density of a small object (or a large one). Many theoretical physicists and astrophysicists are still studying these gravitational objects in relation to other objects. It is sufficiently complex that it can take many years to work through the formulas to answer what would seem like simple questions. Often, we find that the solutions don't match up with our observations. Then we have to ask, is our theory fundamentally wrong, or only in need of small adjustments.

A Student Hacker

The author at the console of the Cornell University Burroughs 220 Computer 1962.

Recollections of a Student Hacker at the Cornell Computer Center, Rand Hall, 1961-1965

When I was an undergraduate student at Cornell University, part of my student financial aid was the opportunity to work at a variety of part time jobs. My sophomore year, 1962-1963, I had a student assistant position as a night operator at the Cornell Computer Center, Rand Hall. In my Senior year, 1964-1965, by then having considerable computer programming experience, I worked as a programmer for a theoretical physicist on a research project. Many years later I learned that John Rudan had assembled a very nice web site on the history of computing at Cornell, including some personal accounts. There is a link to Dr. Rudan's book, "The History of Computing at Cornell" for which the stories were collected. I wrote an account of my own experiences which as far as I know is still posted there. The following is an edited and updated version.

These notes recount some of my experiences as a student at Cornell, both as a part time employee of the Computer Center through student financial aid, as a student programming for fun, and as a part time employee in a theoretical physics project. At the time I had no idea how much influence this experience would have, but it changed my life in unexpected ways so I have included at the end an account of how my career in biomedical computing came out of this exposure.

When I began my undergraduate studies at Cornell in 1961, I had just begun to learn about computing. It was a secondary interest, not closely related to my interest in mathematics and physics. I found out that the Computer Center provided free student access to its Burroughs 220 computer. I taught myself Burroughs 220 assembly language and began my first programming project, not for a class, but just out of interest in what could be done with computers, other than arithmetic. I and my friend from high school, Eric Marks, had discovered a small book by Lejaren Hiller and Leonard Isaacson, called "Experimental Music". Hiller and Isaacson's work resulted in a composition, "Illiac Suite for String Quartet," named for the computer at the University of Illinois that they used. The goal of Eric's and my project was to replicate some of their experiments in automatically composing music according to rules of harmony, voice leading, and also some more modern composition techniques. I soon realized that neither assembly language nor languages like Algol and FORTRAN were suitable for this task. I did not know at the time that a very powerful programming language called Lisp had just been invented to express exactly these kinds of symbolic, abstract ideas. I also did not

50

know that this kind of programming was called "artificial intelligence." Nevertheless, it was my start. The project was an utter failure. I had endless trouble creating a suitable encoding system for the musical notes, chords, etc. The following year, I was privileged to be offered a part time job as a night operator, through student financial aid. I had two wonderful teachers, Amos Ziegler, and George Petznick. Amos taught me how to operate the Burroughs in a production style, as well as a modest amount of console troubleshooting.

I learned how to put machine language instructions in through the console buttons, as well as write little programs that would flash messages on the 4x10 light arrays of the console registers. Amos taught me how to operate the big tape drives (1-inch wide tape), and I had my own tape for my personal programming experiments.

One of the benefits of the job was that we student operators also got instruction in programming, algorithms and data structures from George Petznick. We met once a week with George. He was a model of clarity, and gave us his best. I am sorry to say, I didn't put the same commitment in. One time, he assigned us to write a sorting algorithm (in FORTRAN) that would sort 100 random integers. I hadn't set aside time to work on it, so at the last minute just before the little class met, I punched up an 8-line program that implemented the simplest thing I could think of, which was, as it turned out, a variant of the bubble sort algorithm. When I presented it in class, George laughed and said it would be very slow. We ran it. It took 8 minutes to do the 100 numbers. George's sort program (the algorithm for which I don't recall, perhaps merge-sort or quicksort) took under 6 seconds.

However, I refused to be embarrassed. My program was horribly inefficient, but it was 100% correct, and it took only a few minutes to write. This set a precedent, which I still follow and teach today, which is to get it right first, and make it efficient afterward.

That year I took Electricity and Magnetism, as well as Applied Mathematics courses, and there were assignments requiring numerical computation. They were not intractable by hand, but one seemed tedious and I thought it could be easily programmed. The problem was to solve an electrostatics boundary value problem by "relaxation." This used the following property of functions that are solutions of Laplace's equation: the value of the function at a point is equal to the average of the values on a boundary surrounding the point. One can start with a crude approximation that matches the boundary values, and then iterates the internal values until the results don't change much in any iteration. I wrote a small program to solve the problem, several days before the homework was due. This one (unlike my first) had lots of errors. I was showing up at the Computer Center, handing a small deck of cards to Amos, which he would very kindly slip into the batch stream, run my job, and bring me back the printout from the IBM 407 line printer (kachunk, kachunk), and I would run off to a quiet place to figure out what was still wrong. After many iterations, I thought I had everything right, but it was ten minutes to class time. I brought my deck to Amos, and he put it in. The line printer printed out intermediate results as the program ran, and as I watched the obviously endless loop, I realized I had forgot to divide by the number of boundary points when computing the average! I wanted to fix it quickly and make one more run, so I could turn in this very "cool" solution to the homework. But Amos had had enough. He said he was just too busy, and chased me out, though kindly. I turned in the incomplete assignment, but I got an A in the course anyway. From that I learned the value of interactive programming.

My next adventure happened during my senior year, when I obtained a part time job as a programmer for a researcher in the Cornell Physics Department.

I am sorry to say I don't remember his name. He was a theorist, doing some numerical calculations applying what was then known as elementary particle phenomenology. From general principles of Quantum Field Theory and some specifics about the known elementary particles, some things could be approximately computed, even though the full theory could not be solved. He wrote a program to compute the pi meson form factor, and asked me to make a few changes and additions. The program, in FORTRAN, ran on the Control Data Corporation 1604 computer. The 1604 was brand new, one of the first computers to use field replaceable printed circuit cards. Unlike the Burroughs, use of the 1604 was not free, and one had to have a University account with real money to which charges would be made. This being a research project, the researcher's grant (perhaps from the National Science Foundation or the Office of Naval Research, I don't remember which) paid for the computer time. However, since I had lots of operator experience, I was able to schedule to come in during the evening and run the CDC 1604 myself. After getting the program into good shape, he asked me to run it for a series of energy transfer values, I think they were something like 1, 5, 10, 25 and 50 GeV. However I got the indexing wrong and the run, which took several hours of chargeable night running time, produced values for 1, 2, 3, 4, 5 GeV instead. When I discovered my mistake, I was so embarrassed I wrote an apology and resignation note, and delivered that and the output to the researcher. He was amused, not angry. His comment was, well, now we have lots of detailed results for the lower energy range. However he accepted my resignation anyway, which was fine because at that point I needed to get caught up on homework and study for final exams.

Actual blank punch-card from 1961

The CDC 1604 was a binary oriented machine with 60-bit words, and octal display registers, as opposed to the Burroughs binary coded decimal organization. One thing that was fun about the CDC was that an amplifier and speaker were attached to one of the register bits, so that you could "hear" the machine (when the bit modification rate was in the audio range…). Of course this led to people writing programs to play music on the console speaker. Remember, this was 1964, well before MIDI and all the wonderful later programs for generating electronic music. However, I was struck by how straightforward this task seemed, compared to the problem of automated music composition, at which I had failed earlier.

I went on to graduate study in theoretical physics at Princeton, and my involvement with computing was dormant until 1978, ten years after completing my Ph.D. I had decided to pursue training in medical physics at the University of Washington Radiation Oncology Department. Within a year or so, I found a niche in the department, because of my prior experience with computing. I wrote some assembly language control programs for a radiation beam scanner. This device had a water tank, motors and ionization chambers to measure radiation beams and was run by a small computer that used a new device called a microprocessor, in which hundreds of thousands of transistors were packed onto a single small silicon chip. Then

I participated in writing an interactive simulation system for designing radiation treatments for cancer (so-called RTP programs).

Radiation Therapy Planning

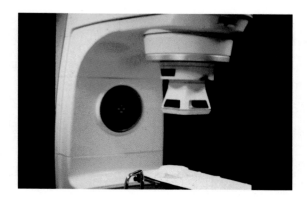

Almost everyone who has cancer will quickly learn that there are three main approaches to treatment of cancer: surgery, radiation and chemo-therapy (broadly speaking, to include immunotherapy as well). My career was devoted to inventing new kinds of software to help plan radiation treatments. In these next few pages, I will explain how this works.

It's not hard to imagine how surgery works. If you can get at the tumor and the local areas where it may have spread, simply removing the mass seems a great approach. The complications are that the surgeon has to get past other body parts and tissues in order to reach the tumor without dam-aging the healthy tissue. When this is impossible, it is said that the tumor is "unresectable". Surgeons depend heavily on knowledge of anatomy and on medical imaging systems, such as CT (computed tomography, a way to get cross sectional images using X-rays), MRI (magnetic resonance imaging, which also produces cross sectional images, but using magnetic fields and radio wave pulses), and PET (positron emission tomography, in which the patient is injected with radioactive atoms that are taken up by the tumor and other tissues, emitting X-rays that can then be used to compute cross sectional images).

Radiation oncologists use digital images in an even more direct way. Two ideas that are central to the success of radiation treatment are: one, with high energy X-ray (photon) beams, not much energy is absorbed by the skin, so patients do not experience terrible skin burns as they did in the early years. The maximum energy from the beam is deposited a few centimeters past the skin, and two, irradiating the tumor from several (or many) different directions insures that a lot of radiation energy goes into the tumor, and the energy absorbed as the beam penetrates to the tumor is spread out to minimize the effects on internal organs, such a lung, liver, heart, gastrointestinal tract and so on.

The goal of radiation therapy planning is to choose and arrange radiation beams for treatment that use these ideas and get sufficient radiation dose into the tumor mass, with as little as possible elsewhere.

Once they have the images for a patient, radiation oncologists use interactive computer programs to display the images, and draw on them where they think the target (tumor and local spread, perhaps to lymph nodes) is. The computer program then shows the radiation beam from a radiation treatment machine, in the same images. Skilled people called "dosimetrists" try different arrangements of radiation beams until they find one that gets lots of radiation energy into the target and not so much in the surrounding. Figure below shows what the computer display looks like for one case, the oval shaped mass in the upper right of the picture, with a line drawn around it.

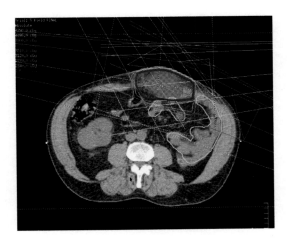

Prism plan 2014

When I started in this field, we used "minicomputers" typically the size of washing machines, or even larger, which had separate display units whose electronics were sometimes as large as the computer. The most popular minicomputer of the 1980s was the VAX series from Digital Equipment Corporation (DEC). At that time, DEC was the second largest computer company in the world, and Microsoft had barely gotten started.

When I became a faculty member, and was faced with the job of writing RTP programs for the UW Radiation Oncology Department, I convinced the department chair, Tom Griffin, to buy a VAX, model 11/780 computer and a graphic display system for the department. I was strongly supported by George Laramore, who also had left a career in theoretical physics, though George actually went to medical school and became a radiation oncologist.

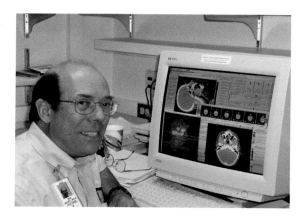

Ira, with treatment plan on screen

In those days, minicomputers cost anywhere between $50,000 and $150,000, and there were only four VAX computers at the University of Washington. Purchasing a computer was quite a process of paperwork and approvals, the UW being a State institution. Each VAX computer was custom built at the DEC factory, according to the requirements of each order, much like passenger jet airplanes today. We placed the order in March 1980, and our DEC sales representative reported that we could expect delivery in nine months.

In the meantime, I had to find a room, get electrical wiring and air conditioning put in, and learn how to manage this minicomputer. The UW Medical Center was very slow about getting this project under way. One of the most important people to contend with was Mrs. Jean Dooley in the hospital materials management department. Despite repeated efforts to convince Mrs. Dooley of the importance of the project, nothing was moving forward .

One morning in December, at about 7 AM, before I had gotten up for breakfast, Alice Striegel called me at home. Alice was the administrative assistant to the department chairman. Alice is one of my favorite people, a very conscientious and hard worker, and one of the nicest people in the department. As I sleepily answered, "Hello?" Alice's voice on the other end queried, "Ira, did you order a computer?" Suddenly I was fully awake. My baby had arrived! "Yes, Alice, I did," I replied. Alice explained that there were a bunch of large cartons, some six feet tall, left in the hallway, and Mrs. Dooley was in the department, stirring up a storm about how this was a violation of the fire regulations. I told Alice I would be there in a jiffy. Skipping breakfast, I threw on some clothes and sped into the hospital. When I arrived, there were all the boxes, and there, indeed was Mrs. Dooley, pacing and fuming. I greeted her, apologized for the problems, and immediately explained how unfortunate this terrible situation was. It just would not be possible to move the boxes into the room designated for the computer, because the electrical wiring and air conditioning were not in yet. I said in my sweetest voice, "Mrs. Dooley, it would be such a tremendous help in solving this fire regulation problem if you could just expedite the electrical and air conditioning work, and then we can get these boxes out of the hallway." In the brief ensuing silence, you could hear a pin drop. Mrs. Dooley quietly assured me she would get right on it.

A few weeks later the room was ready and we got the VAX unpacked and set up. I became the chief cook and bottle washer, programmer, system administrator, etc. In the meantime, I had hired Jonathan Jacky to work with me. Jon had just finished a postdoctoral fellowship in physiology, and like me had a nascent interest in computing. The VAX was a multi-user computer. In other UW departments (physics and chemistry) each computer had sometimes as many as one hundred people simultaneous using the one computer but Jon and I had this VAX all to ourselves!

VAX 780 installed at UW Radiation Oncology Department

Jon Jacky

Jon and I had to quickly get some programs running, and they had to be correct, since the calculations would be used for planning treatment for real patients in the clinic. We wrote programs for managing data that were table driven so that the program itself could be kept simple. The handling of data by these programs was horribly inefficient (sound familiar?) but we got the whole set running in 7 months, complete with interactive display of X-ray cross sectional images. The design of the data entry program and the overall design of the whole suite were innovative and warranted publication in computing research journals, so the class with George Petznick was the first link to my newly emerging career in computing.

Meanwhile, I became acquainted with Steve Tanimoto and Alan Borning at the UW Computer Science Department. From Steve and Alan, I learned about artificial intelligence (AI), and together with Computer Science graduate student Witold Paluszynski, began to work on innovative applications of artificial intelligence to the radiation treatment planning problem.

Artificial Intelligence

Of course in the meantime I learned Lisp, and then I got some perspective on the experimental music project of my freshman year at Cornell. The application of AI to RTP turned out to be far more tractable. It (and other applications of AI in medicine and biology) became the focus of my career, in Biomedical and Health Informatics.

Since then we have gone through many generations of computers and several RTP software projects. The third generation of RTP software we created, the Prism system, runs on very inexpensive desktop or even laptop computers, with Linux, and is written in the Common Lisp programming language. For a time, Jon moved on to Mechanical Engineering where he worked on software for a magnetic resonance force microscope. Later he returned to the Radiation Oncology Department, to complete a software project we started much earlier, a new computerized control system for the UW Clinical Neutron Therapy System.

Meanwhile, George Laramore became the chairman of the Radiation Oncology Department, and continued to strongly support our little group of pioneers in computing in radiation oncology. I am now Professor Emeritus of Radiation Oncology, and also Professor Emeritus of Biomedical Informatics and Medical Education, one of the founders of the University of Washington

Biomedical and Health Informatics graduate program, as well as an adjunct faculty member in the UW Department of Computer Science and Engineering from 1983 until I retired. I wrote a book, called "Principles of Biomedical Informatics," published by Academic Press (Elsevier) in October 2008. The second edition was published in 2013. My computing experiences as an undergraduate at Cornell played a significant role in what has turned out to be a fun and wonderful career. I am grateful to Amos Ziegler and George Petznick for the opportunity they provided to me way back then.

George Laramore

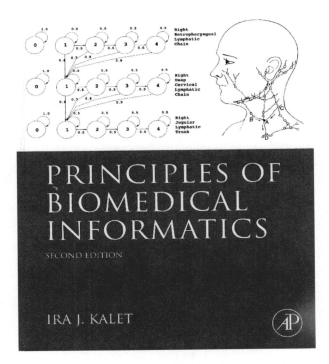

PRINCIPLES OF BIOMEDICAL INFORMATICS

SECOND EDITION

IRA J. KALET

University of Washington, June, 2008 (updated December, 2014)

McTaggart

I grew up on Long Island, near New York City, with an interest in ice hockey, but did not learn to skate as a child. I was a math and science geek, not an athlete. The sport seemed exotic and inaccessible to me until I went to college at Cornell University in upstate New York. There I discovered that the University had an intramural ice hockey program organized so that anyone could learn to play, even if you had not skated before. I signed up, and played through all four years of college. Sometimes, the stick was my "third leg," as my balance was not too good, but over the years I started to get stronger and had lots of fun. I scored one goal the entire four years.

My Junior year, the team on which I played, the Scramblers, came in third out of thirty-two teams. Continuing intramural hockey while I was a theoretical physics graduate student at Princeton, I joined a team of graduate students, and we played teams fielded by the eating clubs. In one game a miracle happened;

I scored twice. After the game I excitedly told our captain, also a physics graduate student, "Norm, I tripled my lifetime goal total in this game." "That's great, Ira," he replied, "We will triple your player salary."

When I came to Seattle, Washington in 1968, there was not much ice hockey and only two ice rinks, so I got involved for many years in other activities, got married, had children, settled into a job as a professor of medical physics at the University of Washington, and not being much of an athlete anyway, that was all good. But ice hockey was not forgotten. In 1992, not having played for 24 years, I got on a team in a local recreational league through a friend. Two years later, that ended as work demands increased. But after another 11-year lapse, in 2005, I decided to try again. I went to an evaluation and draft skating session run by the Greater Seattle Hockey League, the largest league in the Northwest. I was clearly the weakest skater of the 30 or so players who showed up. But the league does its best to get everyone on a team, and I was the next to last to be drafted, to a new team in the beginner's division, called the Hackers, appropriate to my involvement with computers. I was back!

After a few years, I thought I had better get some more formal instruction so, I signed up for a 10-session adult recreational ice hockey camp. It was two nights a week, for 5 weeks, an hour and 15 minutes each session. The program is run by Jim McTaggart, who played in the NHL and has been a local coach for many years. Jamie Huscroft, another former NHL player and local coach also is an instructor in the program. There were about 30 participants at a range of skill levels, from very low intermediate (me) to very high level. Jim and Jamie ran us ragged. I struggled to keep up. I have always been a bit of a timid hockey player. When I got the puck, I would immediately get rid of it, sometimes toward the goal, not necessarily to a teammate. The drills in these classes expected me to skate with the puck, target passes, all things I needed to learn. I was nervous, scared of messing up and having the others laugh at me. Somehow they didn't. I was still there in the last session. For each drill, I waited for my turn, studying the others, struggling just to remember what to do, never mind about doing it well.

The last exercise that Jim had us do was very challenging. At the boards on the side, next to the face-off circle at one corner, was a pile of pucks. Jim had the players each take a turn at picking up pucks and attempting to pass them to the middle in front of the goal, where another player was standing to catch the pucks and take shots at the goalie. The challenge was that yet another player took a turn as an opponent, whose job was to prevent the player with the puck pile from getting the passes through. I was the last in line, and no one was left to be the "opponent" so McTaggart acted as my opponent. Was I terrified? You bet. I tried puck after puck and he just tapped them away. Then he came at me as I picked up a puck and started shoving me to get me off balance. My reaction was visceral. I wasn't going to let him get away with that. I shoved back. I got him out of the way and sent the puck straight to the waiting team mate. And then I did another, he shoved me and I shoved back and got the puck through again. After the third success, our time was up for the night, but I was so charged up I could have kept right on.

It was a transforming moment. Jim was grinning at me. I went home that night feeling for the first time like a real hockey player. Since then I have repeated the same hockey camp, and have also been doing skating lessons. I turned seventy in April 2014. My skill level continued to increase after that first workshop, and I have had more fun than ever, but nothing has done as much for my self-confidence as that night that Jim McTaggart lit a fire in me and got me to take him on. (Ira was registered to attend the April 2015 workshop but died a few days before).

*The author with his new (2005) team jersey
and modern protective equipment.*

Hackers 2008 Ira lower right

I Slept Here

Ira at a Peace Rally in Sonoma

The decade of the Sixties and just beyond was a formative time for me, as a student at Cornell University, followed in 1965 by graduate study in theoretical physics at Princeton University. It was awkward at times to be studying physics with legendary physicists who had worked on the atomic bomb project and on more contemporary military research pertaining to the War in Vietnam. My friends and I divided our time between quantum field theory and anti-war activities. The theoretical physics work is reported in the research journals, so here I will only relate our experiences with politics.

Each of us was on mailing lists of various organizations that would send out notices of events, educational material, calls to write to our Congresspeople, and so on. One day we got the idea that the organizations should all be in touch with each other. So a handful of us graduate students, who at that time shared a rental house in Princeton, started to compile a list of lists of antiwar and other activist groups, containing contact information for all the organizations we personally knew about. We wrote to each asking if they would like to be listed, and if they would like to receive the list in return. The response was overwhelmingly positive, so we put together the first bulk mailing, announcing this new communication channel. Suddenly we realized we had created yet another organization (and of course it had to be listed). We rented a Post Office box in Princeton. Finally came the most difficult challenge of all: we needed a name, so people could easily refer to us. After a lot of brainstorming, I reminded the group of the Committees of Correspondence of American revolutionary war time, and suggested that since we are putting all the other committees (organizations) in touch with each other, we should call ourselves "The Central Committee of Correspondence". We called for contributions to help defray costs, and invited organizations that were not listed but who wished to be added, to contact us. The list grew rapidly. In the process I learned how to operate a mimeograph machine and type on mimeo masters. It was clear that if you want to end the War and stuff, you have to learn practical things like that. It is not enough to just sing along at concerts and show up at rallies.

March on Washington 1963
"Dr. Spock brought us up; we won't go!"

In 1963 a march was organized to protest the war in Viet Nam, and we would walk from Princeton to Washington DC. Along the way, walkers were hosted in many cities and town by supporters who live in those communities.

Along the way, walkers were hosted in many cities and towns by supporters who lived in those communities. At our rented house in Princeton, we graduate students hosted some of the walkers, the two nights they were in town. I was inspired to join them, and left Princeton with the group. We walked through Trenton, staying with families in different locations. As we walked through neighborhoods and business districts, along the way we were greeted by many supporters, and also confronted by angry opponents, who, yes, really threw tomatoes and other stuff at us. After arriving in Philadelphia we spent the night at the Arch St. Friends Meeting, one of the oldest in the US. We slept on the straw cushions in the pews, in the center section of the building. That was far enough for me.

The next day, I took a train back to Princeton. After another day or two I was having horrible pain in my feet. At the Princeton University Infirmary, McCosh Hall, the doctor could not find any injury or other problems. He then asked if I had been doing a lot of walking or running lately. I told him I had walked to Philadelphia. He was visibly annoyed, but assured me I would be fine in a few days or a week, and advised me to stay off my feet for a while. Once I had telephone service in my own name, I began to refuse to pay the Federal telephone excise tax, a tax that the Congress passed specifically to help fund the US involvement in war in Vietnam. Routinely the IRS Collections Division would find some source of funds, typically the payroll office where I worked, and forcibly collect the money anyway, but so many thousands of people were publicly involved that it was an effective way to increase awareness of the war and our complicity as taxpayers. Although this might seem futile, it served as a good talking point in speaking publicly about the war in Vietnam. One time though, it had an impact in a surprising way. I had just started in a faculty position at Sonoma State College in Northern California.

One day I received a call from a woman in the Personnel department. She explained that she was processing the IRS lien for the telephone tax, and wanted to talk with me. I agreed to meet with her in person at her office across campus. Anxious, wondering what I would be dealing with, I found her office and we met. She explained that she needed advice on a personal family matter, and thought I might be able to help because of my involvement in the tax resistance movement. She explained that her son, who was just turning 18, had decided to refuse to register for the draft (the Selective Service System). She was worried about what might happen to him, and also did not understand why he would do something so drastic. I asked about her family's values and religious tradition, their views about conflict and war, and about human life. She said that this conversation was extremely helpful, because she realized that her son was just taking very seriously and thoughtfully the values that his parents had taught him. While she remained anxious about the risks he was taking, she said that she felt much better knowing that what he was doing was something she could support and be proud of.

An Attorney for All Seasons

Brian Kalet and John Caughlin 1978

John Caughlan, Protector, Friend and Inspiration

Heroes can be found in many places, though few attorneys rise to this level. John Caughlan was one of my heroes. He taught us that in the United States we have a system of law, not a system of justice. However, he used his knowledge and experience of the law to help bring justice for many people. John was not Jewish, but if the Torah is a Torah of justice for all, John was a modern Torah sage and leader.

John and his wife, Goldie, had been dear friends of mine for some years, but when I found out that an agent from the Intelligence Division of the U.S. Internal Revenue Service was investigating me, John became my attorney of record. As I mentioned I had been involved for some time with the movement to protest the war in Vietnam by refusing to pay the federal excise tax on telephone service. However, when I took next steps to refuse income tax as well, my case went to the Intelligence Division, to determine whether the Federal Government should pursue prosecution. Thus I learned about a young man I will just call "Inspector Javert," since I don't recall his real name.

At some point, Inspector Javert requested to meet with me to answer some questions. I agreed to meet with him at John's office, and he appeared there at the appointed time. I asked Inspector Javert if he would mind if I asked him a few questions, before he began his interrogation. He was very polite and patient. I asked about his college studies, his major and his interests, and how he came to work for the IRS. It was his first job offer, and a very good one financially. I asked him if he was aware of how horrible and unnecessary, even undesirable the U.S. military action in Vietnam was. He didn't venture a personal opinion of course, but continued to listen politely as I explained why people were protesting and even refusing to pay their taxes. Finally, I paused and he asked, "Do you have any more questions?" I said I didn't and thanked him very much for his patience and cooperation. Then he said, "So, now it is my turn?" I responded, "Yes, certainly." He then explained, "I know this seems redundant but I have to ask and record everything, so can you please confirm that your name is indeed 'Ira J. Kalet?'" I took a deep breath. Then I apologized profusely. I said, "I know you have been very patient and you are just trying to do the job assigned to you, but my attorney, Mr. Caughlan, has advised me not to answer any questions, on the grounds that the answers could be used to incriminate me." His disappointment was palpable. He replied, "So, I guess we are done?" "Yes," I said. I added that I hoped he would find a better job someday which did not require him to be in such a difficult position, and we said cordial "Goodbyes." No other attorney I knew could have helped me prepare for that encounter.

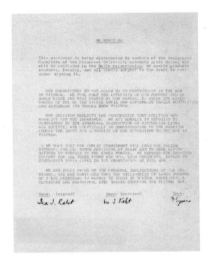

I was never prosecuted. The war ended, as everyone knows, and eventually the Collections Division got any and all back taxes they thought I owed, with penalties and interest, but in the meantime we all learned a lot from this drama. Some years later, but way too soon, John passed away. I was only one of many people whose lives he had touched, and I was privileged to speak at a memorial for him. Here are my comments from that very sad day.

John Caughlan was for me the ideal of the legal profession. He was a seeker, a person with a vision of creating a civilized society. His work as an attorney was a part of his effort to bring about that civilization. He did not see his work as just a job but as a part of a whole and integrated life.

We knew each other for many years, and it is not possible to express all the wonderful times in a few words. Two things we shared will have to suffice.

John agreed to be my legal counsel when I decided to refuse to pay Federal income taxes or file returns, at the height of the US government's war in Vietnam. I was one of a small but growing group of war protestors. When I learned that I was being investigated for criminal prosecution by an agent in the IRS Intelligence Division, I decided to get assistance. Most attorneys with whom I spoke were eager to "get me off," to protect their client from harm. They did not understand that my personal welfare was not my main concern, but that I wanted to use the conflict for public and private education about war and governments. John understood this. He saw the higher purpose, and guided me skillfully and as a real friend through the encounters with the IRS agent, and later with US Attorney Irwin Schwartz, and others at the IRS. When they tried to impugn my motives, John helped set them straight, and helped me point out their complicity in the Vietnam war. It was scary, as after all, I did risk prosecution and prison, but it was fun and exhilarating to be with someone with that vision of a better world.

Later, in our leisure time, John and I went hiking and mountain climbing in the Cascades. John was a wonderful companion. We were both pretty amateur, and try as we might we still made mistakes, though not too serious. Once, while enroute up Ingalls Peak, I was above John. I knocked loose a small rock, which hit him in the arm and left a nasty bruise. I feel guilty to this day. Another time, we were in the small cirque above Monte Cristo, called Glacier Basin, and this time John was above me. He kicked loose a small avalanche, which scared the daylights out of me, but it stopped well short of me. Fortunately, he was in no danger. Well, the truth is, I think that in some more spiritual sense, John was always above me, setting a great example for me to climb higher. Now his memory will have to suffice for us all to continue the climb.

Superstitious Hooey

My father, Ben Kalet came to live with us for the last few months of his life. As he slowly declined and slipped into unconsciousness we sat with him.

As Shabbat approached we anticipated saying goodbye to him. Our family assembled in the dining room and Terry lit the candles. There was an emptiness as we felt Ben's absence from the table. It didn't seem right to say Kiddush without him. We gathered up the Kiddush cup and challah and assembled around the bed with our three sons. By the time I finished blessing the children, Ben had opened his eyes, and by the time we had finished Kiddush he was sitting on the edge of the bed and was ready to get up. He joined us for diner at the dinning room table and ate a hearty meal.

By early December, Ben was no longer able to get out of bed, or even stay in bed. When he fell out of bed one evening, we accepted his inevitable transfer to Evergreen Hospice. He had some awareness and could talk but not much. Referring to the hospice facility he said, "This is some nice hotel. "Once again, he became apparently unconscious. The first night of Chanukah arrived, and we brought a hanukkiah to his bedside. The hospice staff gave their OK to light the candles. We had no idea if he was aware of us. His eyes were closed. We lit the candles and began to sing the blessings. Part way through, his eyes opened and he was able to smile. On the second night he remained asleep and during the second day he was gone. As we light the Shabbat candles each week, and as we approach his yahrzeit on the second day of Chanukah each year I am reminded of power of Shabbat and the fragility of life and light.

The author and a Hanukkiah made from an old wooden ice hockey stick.
The jersey is a replica jersey of the Israel National Ice Hockey team.

The Content's the Thing

D'var Torah
Shabbat Shuvah, 5753
Temple B'nai Torah Mercer Island, Washington

Shabbat Shuvah, the Sabbath of Turning, is one of the two occasions on which the Eastern European rabbis traditionally gave long sermons, the other being Shabbat Ha-Gadol, before Pesach. Perhaps this was to make up for the fact that they did not otherwise give sermons to their congregations. Arthur Green explains the tradition further in a commentary in the book, "The Jewish Holidays," by Michael Strassfield, while the Shabbat Ha-Gadol sermon was lengthy because of the details of Passover to be explained, the sermon on Shabbat Shuvah was to serve as a *hit'orerut li-te-shuvah*, an impassioned call for repentance. It was offered amid tears and wailing, and was so delivered as to wring dread and compassion from the most stone like heart… the prayer books for the ten days of penitence are filled with parables and simple homilies about people who were led astray by their vices, were punished for their sins, and returned to God in contrition and tears.

According to tradition, then, I have two obligations, first to terrify you all into returning to the ways of God, and second, to speak at great length. I do not intend to meet either of these obligations. Indeed, the Torah portions for the two previous weeks have already treated this subject more adequately than I could aspire to do.

Instead I would like to devote some brief comments to this week's Torah portion, *Vayalech,* which tells of Moses passing on leadership to Joshua, and of hearing from God that the Jewish people will continue their struggle to follow God's mitzvot, failing and returning again.

I call your attention to Chapter 31, verse 9, which says, "Moses wrote down this Teaching and gave it to the priests, sons of Levi, who carried the Ark of the Lord's Covenant, and to all the elders of Israel." In this verse, "Teaching" refers to the entire Torah, not just to the book of *D'varim,* or the song that follows in Chapter 32.

Why is it so important to write down this Teaching? There are three explanations, two from the text and one not so apparent. The first and obvious explanation is in the next few verses, namely, so that it may periodically be read to the people, that they may learn, remember and observe faithfully.

The second explanation, mentioned in verse 19 and reiterated by Moses in verse 26, is that the Torah will serve as God's witness against the people of Israel. When we stray from the path, God may be hidden, but the written Torah remains as a witness to the Covenant, as the recorded contract, so to speak. We can not plead that our memories failed us, nor that we were not given guidance in all these matters.

The third explanation is not so apparent here. I believe the "writing down" responds to a question, "How do we know that God really appeared to Moses?" Well, that may not be exactly the question you are wondering about, so, let me put it another way, "On what basis do we accept and observe the commandments?" This is not an easy question for many of us, who do not simply accept the dictum that the Torah is the Word of God and that is that.

The answer is to be found in the Torah itself. In *Sh'mot* (Exodus) Chapter 4, when God called Moses to lead the people of Israel out of Egypt, Moses pleaded that he was slow of speech and slow of tongue. And this was God's reply: "Who gives one speech? Who makes him dumb or deaf, seeing or blind? Is it not I, the Lord? Now go, and I will be with you as you speak and will instruct you what to say." So it is not in how Moses spoke, nor in external authority, but in the content itself that we can discern the divine inspiration.

We are Israel, we struggle with God. Just as the ideas and theories of science are not simply accepted on authority but must stand up to critical examination, we are constantly questioning and examining the teachings of Torah, testing their meaning and significance in light of our experience and intuition.

The narrative, the action, the characters of the Torah are frank, realistic. The Torah pulls no punches, but tells tales of deceit and loyalty, love and hate, life and death, the range of human conditions. It is not a sanitized account. But from each story, sentence and word, we can learn how to live better.

And so, generation after generation, the Torah stands on its own merits. The written words of the Torah are there for us to examine and turn over, and for us to enjoy and love, as Ben Bag Bag said, "Turn it over and over, for it contains everything. Keep your eyes riveted to it. Spend yourself in its study. Never budge from it, for there is no better way of life than that."

And now to return to Moses...

Moses is a reflection of us, for like the "defiant and stiff-necked" people he led, he was far from perfect. There was the incident of the murder of the

Egyptian; Moses himself doubted and argued with God (as is our tradition); he was guilty of slander... in all, the Midrash tells us that Moses transgressed not once, not twice, but six times.

Yet Moses wanted passionately for his people to fulfill their destiny, for its own sake, for *kedushah*.

We, too, are far from perfect. But we can aspire to *kedushah*. And, notwithstanding the terrifying narrative of blessings and curses, for me the real motivation is that a life devoted to justice, compassion, love, learning, building, exploring and teaching is a good life, that these things are worth doing for their own sake.

Our community has that devotion, as a community and on the part of each individual. So, as we approach Yom Kippur, I pray that we are sealed in the Book of Life for a good year, not only so we may enjoy the sweets of ordinary life, but also so that we may turn our devotion into action, and further the process of *tikkun olam*. May it be God's will that we live to do God's will.

Time and T'shuvah

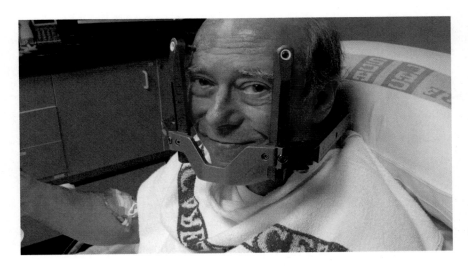

Ira in gamma knife halo prior to treatment of brain metastasis

D'var Torah
Yom Kippur, Fall 5764
University of Washington Hillel
Seattle, Washington

In 2003, I spent fifteen days as an inpatient at the University of Washington Medical Center, receiving Interleukin-2 (IL-2) treatment for metastatic kidney cancer. It overlapped Passover, and I asked the hospital dietary staff if they could provide meals that were Kosher for Passover. They made a heroic effort, and found a supply of frozen packaged meals, which they prepared. Alas, they were way too salty for someone like me who now had only one kidney and was already retaining fluid from the IL-2 treatment. Rabbi Dan Bridge, then serving as the Rabbi and Executive Director of the Hillel Foundation for Jewish Life at the University of Washington, heard about it and brought me a plate of fresh food from the Hillel Passover lunch program. It was the best meal I have ever had in any hospital, and visiting with Dan was a wonderful gift in addition. Subsequently, he asked me how having cancer had changed my life, my perception of things, and invited me to be the guest *Darshan* (commentator on the Torah) for the Yom Kippur morning service at Hillel. Here are my comments.

Each year as Yom Kippur approaches, in accordance with our tradition, I have agonized over my mistakes of the previous year, indeed my whole life up to that point, with remorse and sadness, but without really understanding the meaning of *teshuva*. A year and a half ago, May, 2002, something happened to me that changed everything. Yes, the big "C," cancer. I learned that I had a very large and very malignant mass in my left kidney. The urologic surgeon quickly made arrangements to remove it. Suddenly I was facing the possibility of imminent death, with little time to spare. Was my life insurance paid up? Would my family be able to survive without me? Would the new graduate program at the UW whose founding I led be able to continue without me? I started to redirect all my energy to making these things OK, not to finish, but to bring things to a state where people could carry them on. I was thinking of Rabbi Tarfon, who used to say (Pirkei Avot, Chapter 2, verse 21), "You are not required to complete the work, yet you are not free to neglect it." Thus began the transformation of my perception of time and my relationship with it.

By Yom Kippur last year, I had made a great recovery, was back at work and feeling better than ever, except for the looming prospect that there was metastatic disease. I began to make long term plans again, and I began to waste time, as I had done so much in the past. But in February, I was shaken once again. The small lesions in my lungs were growing, and a thoracoscopic biopsy in March confirmed that they were metastatic renal cell cancer. Now I was in for a course of heavy-duty immunotherapy, Interleukin-2, for three weeks, and as it turned out, it overlapped Pesach. It was a wild ride, which I survived with the enormous help of so many family and friends, including Rabbi Dan, that it would take the rest of the day to name them all. For the time being, it appears that the IL-2 treatment has been effective. However, the course of kidney cancer is very unpredictable. Not only can there be spontaneous resumption of metastatic growth, but also spontaneous remission. Thus, I will be living a life of explicit uncertainty, punctuated by periodic visits to the X-ray CT scanner.

From these experiences, I have come to realize there is one really subtle sin that challenges us, that dogs us all the days of our lives, and that is the sin of thinking we will live forever. This leads us to waste time, to pass up opportunities, thinking we can do it next week or next year. Perhaps I will live to 80, or even more, but now I well know that I might not. I still make long term plans, but not unrealistically long term, and only the plans I consider most meaningful and special to me. I have had to think about what is most important each day, and how to build and lead without cultivating dependency. I am learning to say "no" to things that are not so important. I am still saying "yes" to doing my share of the housework, but without resentment, and without delay. It is no longer a question of avoiding sin in the usual sense, but of making each day and each week a meaningful one, to be able on Shabbat to say, "The week may have been easy or it may have been hard, but regardless, I did with it what I could."

This Yom Kippur, I cannot afford to look back and fill my day with remorse. While I say, *"al chet,"* I mean "what will I do this year, with this rare gift that has been given me, to live a little longer." When Rabbi Eliezer says (Pirkei Avot, Chapter 2, verse 15), "repent one day before your death," I believe he meant, "Do not let this day's opportunity to live to the fullest go by, for it will not come again."

Agreement for the Sake of Heaven

The D'var Torah
Shabbat Emor, 5764
(May 8, 2004)
Congregation Beth Shalom Seattle, Washington

An old saying, "two Jews, three opinions," captures well our love of argument and discussion. Tevye, the central character in the musical and film, "Fiddler on the Roof," argues with himself. The Talmud painstakingly records all the discussion of the Oral Torah, including even the dissenting opinions of the Sages, as well as the later commentators. On the other hand, at times in Jewish history, periods of diversity have also generated much antagonism, which can take centuries to resolve. Today, the community indeed lives in a period of diversity, not always peacefully. I took the opportunity in the commentary here to address this problem. A family story and a transcript of a dialog with a friend develop the idea further.

Two years ago I learned that I had a nasty kidney tumor. A big surgery, two small ones, and two courses of Interleukin-2 therapy followed. Many, including Rabbi Gartenberg, have been wonderful to me and Terry during this challenging time. I cannot thank you enough for your prayers, good wishes, food, company, and patience. It appears to have had a good effect. At the present time I have no remaining detectable disease. That does not mean I am cured, but it means that for now I am going to redirect my efforts to things and people I neglected of late. So, I will not be speaking today about my battle with cancer, or about cancer in general. However, I do want to take this opportunity to talk about another personal matter. As a dutiful darshan, I will start with the *parasha,* but as this is a *derash,* it will twist and stretch the text to make a point.

Last week's parasha, Kedoshim, and the Haftarah, from Amos, present contrasting views of Israel. Rabbi Gartenberg drew our attention to the commentary of Michael Fishbane, who points out that Kedoshim posits a special place and role for Israel, "You shall be holy, as I, the Lord your God, am holy," while Amos says that we are no different than the other nations. Fishbane's brief text is a challenge to resolve these views.

Parashat Emor also deals with two kinds of topics. The laws to be followed by the priests carry the theme of separation, or specialness, contrasting with the observance of Shabbat and the festivals, in which everyone participates together. But is it a different kind of distinction? I think we can find a common thread here. The priests act only on behalf of the people. If they are not part of *klal yisrael,* their duties and special role have no meaning. Here too, the specialness and the commonality must be linked and harmonized somehow.

Now what has this to do with me, personally? I went to Hebrew school at a Conservative synagogue on Long Island, not in the same neighborhood as the public schools I attended. Like so many other young people at that time, I developed no sense of connection to the Jewish community, and left after becoming a bar mitzvah. It was only many years later, with my wife Terry's urging, that I reconnected, and we joined Temple B'nai Torah. We got thoroughly involved. At the same time, through our friends and through Terry's involvement in Jewish education, as Education Director at Temple B'nai Torah and later at Congregation Beth Shalom, we also turned up at the Conservative and Orthodox synagogues, as well as at Chabad, Seattle Kollel activities, and many secular Jewish community events. One of the most wonderful things Terry did was to bring together educators from all different parts of the community, to teach the children. About a third of the teachers who worked with her were Reform, a third Conservative and a third Orthodox. Terry based her efforts on the model she saw in the programs of the Seattle Jewish Education Council. The good will and cooperation was amazing. At the same time, I heard other people from each group within the Jewish community make the most disparaging comments about the other groups.

Yes, there is plenty to criticize, in every sector, from ultra-secular to ultra pious. But it has bothered me for some time. Even within each group, within even a single shul, one can hear lots of judgmental comments, so-and-so is excessively pious, so-and-so is not serious, and categorical assertions along the same lines. It stands in stark contrast to the non-judgmental attitude of the wonderful people who worked with Terry to further Jewish education. Making distinctions is a central theme in the Torah, between holy and ordinary, between Shabbat and the other days, between Israel and the other nations. But it must be done with a base of agreement. When we are able to identify that on which we agree, we can begin to disagree about the rest. If we do not have a solid base of agreement, the disagreement has no purpose.

In Pirke Avot, chapter 5, verse 21, we read, "Every dispute for the sake of Heaven (machaloket l'shem shamayim) will stand, while a dispute not for the sake of heaven will not stand."

The disputes between Hillel and Shammai stood on a common base, the desire to learn how to live a meaningful Jewish life. The rebellion of Korach was based only on a desire for power. I digress to tell a story. A new rabbi was at his first Shabbat service for his new shul. When they reached the Sh'ma Yisrael prayer, half the congregation stood up and the other half remained seated. Each called to the other to stand up, or sit down. After the service, a representative of each group went to the new rabbi, to argue that his group represented the minhag (custom) of the shul. The new rabbi went in desperation to the old rabbi, now retired, along with the two congregants. The first congregant said to the old rabbi, "Rabbi, isn't it our custom that we stand up when we say the Sh'ma?". The old rabbi shook his head saying, "No, that is not the tradition." The second congregant, somewhat elated, then said, "So, Rabbi, it's really our custom that we sit when we say the Sh'ma?" Again, the old rabbi replied, "No, that is not the tradition." At this, the new rabbi said, completely exasperated, "Rabbi, with all respect, they can't both be right. Half of them are standing up, half are sitting down, everyone is yelling and I can't hear myself pray. "The old rabbi nodded his head and affirmed, "Yes, that is the tradition."

But wait, this is actually a "machaloket l'shem shamayim". On what did both groups agree? They were committed to reciting the Sh'ma, together as a community. Sometimes we take for granted the agreements, and we are surprised or disturbed when we find our assumptions were wrong, or excessive. That is not the time to say, "yes, but…" Instead, we have to listen and look more carefully, to reestablish a common understanding. My challenge to all of you is to see through our disputes, within Congregation Beth Shalom, within the Conservative movement, among the Reform, Conservative, Orthodox, and other Jewish branches, and even with the rest of the world, to identify and reaffirm that on which we agree. Only then can we begin to discuss our differences.

To start off the process, I will offer an idea of Rabbi Ken Zisook, Orthodox rabbi, formerly of Seattle, later a congregational rabbi in Fredrickton, New Brunswick, Canada. Rabbi Zisook says that one thing the entire Jewish community has in common and can do together is to study Torah. To do that, each has to set aside their judgmental opinions about the other. Rabbi Zisook once said that a serious Orthodox Jew has more in common with a serious Reform Jew than he/she does with a non-serious Orthodox Jew. Let's see if this is conceivable. What follows is an excerpt from the introduction to each of three chumashim, Reform, Conservative and Orthodox (not necessarily in that order). Can you guess which is which?

"The Torah is the foundational sacred text of Judaism; the study of its words and their meaning is at the core of Jewish religious experience."

"The Torah is… Israel's distinctive record of its search for God. It… records… the meeting of the human and the Divine, the great moments of encounter."

"The Torah is the eternal, living monument of God's rendezvous with Israel, the nation's 'raison d'etre', the soul that enables the nation to... rise to undreamed of spiritual heights..."

Yes, these introductions also include lots of matters on which they take divergent paths. If the paths are to ever join or even connect, much work is to be done. But this is not the first time Judaism has seen diversity. In Rabbi Jacob Neusner's text, "The Way of Torah," he traces the historical development of Judaism and describes periods of diversity and periods of unity. Throughout there is one constant, the Torah. If Judaism has a future it will not come from one group triumphally imposing its views on the others. It will come from the continuing commitment we all have, of Ahavat Torah, and of Talmud Torah Lish'ma. Now, to that we must all start to add other points of agreement. If you can't find any, then create them. What do I mean by "create them?" It is this: if you re-examine your own ideas and opinions, you may find that you can stretch and reach toward others with a more open mind. Take a chance, and they might just do the same for you. This is once again the great Torah principle of "Love your neighbor as yourself".

Which brings us back to our parashiot. As we review the details of holiday observances set forth in parashat Emor, and especially as we count up to Shavuot, we are challenged to reconnect with the rest of the community, to stand together with the kahal on common ground, and in doing so, insure the future of klal Israel and the Torah.

Unexpected Differences — Two Family Stories

My mother's two brothers, my Uncle Leo and Uncle Harold, were very dear to me. Uncle Leo, Aunt Viola and my cousins Nina and Anitra lived next door to my grandparents, in a then very rural area in Suffolk County, Long Island. My parents could not afford to send us kids to camp, but many Summers we were able to spend a week or two with my grandparents. My brother Stephen and I loved the pie crust my grandmother made, and often were caught nibbling at the edges before the filling was ready. One time my grandmother decided it was hopeless and baked an entire pie crust just for the two of us to eat, without any filling. That was 60 years ago, but I can still taste it in my memory. Uncle Leo had one hundred acres of blueberry bushes behind the houses. Every Summer that we were there at harvest time, he would pay us a dollar for each "flat" of blueberries we picked and brought back to the barn. It was wonderful not only as a way to earn a little spending money, but it happens that blueberries are my favorite fruit, so some small percentage of the harvest never made it to the barn...

Uncle Leo owned a very successful landscaping business. He was always kind to me and my brother and sisters, teased us but also taught us. He was passionate about golf and knew many of the professional golfers at that time. Uncle Harold, Aunt Esther and their daughter, my cousin Carol, lived in Cold Spring Harbor, and we saw them less often, but I was also very fond of them. Uncle Harold was a clinical psychologist and taught at Hofstra College.

Harold shared Leo's passion for golf, and they seemed very close. One time they took me to a golf driving range, hoping to teach me a little about the game. I went through an entire bucket of balls. The farthest any ball went was about 25 feet. It was a hopeless case if ever there was one.

Nina and Anitra are a little older than me, and we did not have so much in common back then, but in recent years Anitra and I have gotten back in touch, and shared memories of our parents and other family members. Anitra told me that when Leo and Harold talked about golf they got along great, but if ever they got started on politics, they would soon become embroiled in loud and intense arguments and disagreements. Anitra explained that this was because Leo was a Socialist and Harold was a Communist.

All these years I had no inkling of it, as neither ever talked about politics with me. Now, from my own generally Left-wing perspective, this too was a "machaloket l'shem shamayim," though perhaps someone from a Right wing perspective would say, all those Lefties are alike.

Harold (left)   Leo (right) Pivnick

It is often said that to get along, people should never discuss politics or religion. Having covered politics, my second family story is about religion.

My wife Terry's family is Catholic. Her father died when she was young, but she maintained a relationship with her paternal grandmother, Minnie Steele, and her Aunt Sally, who lived with Minnie in an apartment on First Hill in Seattle. My very first visit to meet Terry's grandmother and aunt was cordial and gracious on their part. On learning that I was Jewish, Minnie said, "Oh, we have several of your people living here in the building. They are very nice; we enjoy them and regard them highly." I thought the use of the expression "your people" in this context was a bit quaint, but charming. I felt sure that Minnie wanted to put me at ease and assure me that I was welcome in their family. Each time we visited, Minnie gave me an update on how her Jewish friends were doing, and her use of the expression, "your people," became a routine part of the conversation, something like the "running gag" in a television show. But it was always meant well. Both Grandmother Minnie and Aunt Sally have passed on, but I retain fond memories of their kindness.

After Terry and I got married, we traveled to my parents' home on Long Island, where I had grown up. Very few of my family members were able to be at our wedding in Seattle, so my Mom organized a big reception at home for my extended family, to meet Terry and celebrate our marriage. It was the usual large family gathering, with lots of happiness, lots of gossip, and lots of food. My grandmother (my father's mother) would speak only Yiddish in Terry's presence, though the rest of my family were very welcoming. In particular, my Aunt Jeannie, my father's baby sister, spent some time talking with Terry, mentioning her two daughters, my cousins Hilary and Melissa. When Terry told Aunt Jeannie about her family background, Aunt Jeannie, in an effort to make Terry feel accepted, blurted out, "Oh, my daughter married one of your people!" It was even more amusing when Terry found out he (the husband) was a Presbyterian. "NOT one of MY people," Terry commented later. It seems that in every walk of life we find diversity and the variety of disputes that arise from it.

Ira and Terry's grandmother Millie Hackett Steele 1973

Hazel Kalet Marshall, Millie and Rose Kalet 1973

Halacha and Diversity in Judaism

Barry Werner

Barry Werner is a fellow medical physicist and also Jewish. During the time he was working in Seattle, we had stimulating conversations about Judaism, the Jewish people and Israel. The conversations continued by email when Barry moved to New Jersey. In one such exchange, reproduced here, Barry's friend Sol raised some provocative questions about Halacha and the Jewish movements or divisions of today. These too seemed to me questions worth wrestling over. The email exchange is from December, 1996, and the subject is "Pluralism".

"Barry, thanks for forwarding the message from your colleague Sol, and your reply, which I think was articulate and accurate.

"On the issue Sol raises about the sense in which the various movements are "halachic," there seems to be a difference between the positions of the Conservative and Reform rabbis as a group. The Conservative Rabbinical Assembly indeed sees itself as an authoritative body for the movement, in regard to Jewish law, and so they made a decision that driving to the shul on Shabbat was permitted, and they expected in general that the membership should follow their decisions (also similar decisions regarding kashrut, etc.). The Reform Central Conference of American Rabbis claims no halachic authority and on these matters they take the approach that they are an advisory body, whose job is to respond carefully to questions, and to educate their members. Many volumes of Reform Responsa have been published. Of course, they also would like the Reform movement membership to adopt their recommendations, but they do not take the position that they are enforceable.

"Now, if you look at actual practice, you understand that the Reform rabbis are right on the question of authority. Many members of Orthodox shuls drive not only to shul on Shabbat but other places too, and their level of observance varies widely. Similarly, Conservative and Reform. In practice, all Jews do the mitzvot that they find meaningful and ignore or violate the ones that they can not or will not adopt. "Statistically, I think you would find that the numbers of people and number of mitzvot show a different distribution in the three movements, with ritual mitzvot statistically much more practiced in the Orthodox, less so in Conservative, and least in Reform. On the other hand, statistically if you examine the ethical mitzvot (and let us not forget that these are as important or more so than the ritual ones) you may find a more uniform or even an inverse distribution. I am impressed with the extent to which members of my Reform synagogue contribute regularly to food banks and to Mazon. This includes every kid who becomes a bar or bat mitzvah. We teach them that it is an obligation to give *tzedaka,* not just something that makes you feel good. Before coming to the Kol Nidre service each year, our membership makes an extra effort on the food drive, and each year since we started this, we collect several tons of food, and about $4,000. In the words of Isaiah, "Is this not the fast that I ask of you?" Is this not halacha?"

Sol posed a question that I surmise comes from essentially an Orthodox perspective, as did his other comments. Here is his question and my response.

"...there have been times when it has been difficult because when you make decisions according to halacha, your immediate emotional desires are not always met. Does this ever happen in the other movements?"

[my response]

"Of course. Every kid would rather keep all his gift money, would rather not do work in the community. What a question!"

Sol continued with a concern that I noted in the D'var Torah in this chapter.

"...I am, however, a bit amazed at the level of negativity directed at the Torah observant community by some others here. I would be interested to ask those who have expressed such negativity: Does it really grow out of personal experience, or is it the result of news reports, speeches from spokespersons, etc.?"

I confess that Sol's comments "pushed one of my buttons" and here is my somewhat petulant response:

"I resent the self-serving use of the term "Torah observant," as if liberal Jews were not trying their best to be Torah observant. The disagreement is about what we should be doing. But Sol's comment carries with it the assertion that the "Torah observant" community is right and the rest are misguided or willfully wayward. Yes, it comes directly from personal experience. But I have to add also that I do not condemn all the Orthodox movement, or its membership. Most people I know personally are doing their best, and as Sol said, are not at all negative towards the rest of us. Just a small example, according to my wife, who is the director of our religious school, 30% of the teachers in our Reform religious school are Orthodox, and some additional percentage Conservative. They are wonderful teachers, they love the kids, they have no problem with the context, and we love them too."

Sol's next question is one I have heard from others, and my response only barely begins to address it. He asks:

"…There are many instances where halacha has been modified by the movements to be more lenient, are there any recent changes that actually place more stringent requirements on the membership?"

At this point I was in full stride.

"If the interpretation of Torah has become so buried in extensions and restrictions and there is a pressing need to revitalize and re-examine whether we have overbuilt "siyag la Torah" (Pirke Avot 1:1), a fence around the Torah, one would not demand or expect some kind of artificial "even-handed" approach, balancing a list of leniencies with a new list of stringencies. But I think the question (and the whole context) is really about the idea that there should be some kind of authority and it should have the power to decide and enforce the law. Moreover that the law should be stringent and onerous. Seems more Catholic than Jewish. Is the Chief Rabbi some kind of Pope?

"In my view, we should rejoice at every mitzvah that anyone does, and stop being so condemning and punitive about the ones we are not yet doing. Especially we should stop condemning people who are not doing ritual mitzvot. Yes, actually we should condemn people who violate the prohibition against murder, and some others as well."

There is a principle that as I understand it, when there is a difference in interpretation of halacha among communities, you follow the practice of the community you are in. An example is: in Tractate Brachot, it is said that two (men) are sufficient to do the zimun before the birchat hamazon, though in the case of three, it is required. In most communities they follow the practice that if there are only two, the zimun is omitted. What do they say of a community in which the practice is to say the zimun when there are only two? Would they (the first) condemn such a practice? Yet, the strident voices among the Orthodox do condemn anything deviating from the practices of their own community as "against halacha". The effect of Orthodoxy in the last hundred years or so is to stifle dissent or deviation, and in the last decades it has gotten worse, to where some of these voices have committed slander and even murder (in particular the murder of Israeli Prime Minister Yitzhak Rabin in 1995 by a young man, an Orthodox zealot). Is that halacha?

Now I do not want to make excuses for any dumb things that some Reform rabbi said, nor should it be necessary to apologize for the incredible things the Reform movement did in the past, like the famous shrimp feed, and I will just say that I don't expect my Orthodox friends to apologize for some of the dumb things that some Orthodox rabbis do, either. The most important thing is that, if we are serious, we should come to Torah with an open mind, united in our interest to discern from it how to fulfill God's will, and tolerant and compassionate and respectful of each other as equals in our effort to learn, and accepting that we are diverse and often disagree. Isn't disagreement and discussion the heart of this kind of learning? I try to keep in mind the words of Ben Zoma, "Who is wise? The one who learns from every person." (Pirke Avot, beginning of Chapter 4)

To this point, I have related for you Sol's voice and mine, but Barry then added the following:

"...I believe that the leaders of the Orthodox movement have intentionally stifled the halachic process in order to frustrate the attempts of the reformers to introduce changes."

At this point I decided to be more brief. It was Friday, and I had taken the better part of the morning with this correspondence, so just added a few more comments.

"In Michael Meyer's book, "Response to Modernity," Meyer documents clearly how little the early reformers wanted to change and how vitriolic the response was from the rabbinic power structure of the time. Polarization continued until it got way out of hand. Now we are picking up the pieces.

Well, it is 11 AM here, and I need to get some writing done for my day job, before Shabbat. So, let me wish you a Shabbat Shalom, whether you drive or not, and of our discussions we will say, "to be continued". All the best, Ira"

And, having passed this long discussion on to you, the reader, I hope you will have the pleasure of continuing it as well.

In conjunction with the Union of American Hebrew Congregations annual meeting in July 1883, a group organized a banquet, among other things to celebrate the first graduating class from Hebrew Union College. The meal included shrimp, crab and clams, and a dairy dessert (the meal also included beef). There was much finger-pointing as to who was to blame, whether it was a mistake of the caterers, or an intentional statement about kashrut. An article in Commentary magazine (search the World Wide Web for "trefa banquet") in 1966 reviews the events and the controversy that followed. The most significant result was that a more tradition-leaning faction within the Reform movement left, and this was the beginning of the Conservative movement.

Jews in Sports

The D'var Torah
Shabbat Emor, 5766 (May 13, 2006)
Congregation Beth Shalom
Seattle, Washington

The commentary following gives a very different take on *parashat Emor* than in the previous chapter. A dialog with a friend around the same time provided an opportunity to delve a little deeper.

The last time I had an opportunity to share a few words of Torah was around this same time of year, also on *parashat Emor*, two years ago. In *Pirke Avot*, Chapter 5, verse 26, "Ben Bag Bag says, turn it (the Torah) and turn it, for everything is in it." Indeed, the *parasha* is inexhaustible. *Parashat Emor* begins with the laws of the *Kohen*, and in particular the *Kohen Gadol*. It continues with further details concerning the offerings. Next, a single long chapter (Lev. 23), covers the entire cycle of communal observances, starting with Shabbat, then Pesach, the Omer, Shavuot, Rosh HaShana, Yom Kippur, Sukkot and *Shemini Atzeret*. Next is a brief mention of the *Ner Tamid*, the Showbread and laws concerning the blasphemer. Quite a lot to choose from. But actually, I am not going to talk about any of that. Today I will begin with Jews in Sports.

Even a cursory look through the collection of short biographies in *Great Jews in Sports*, by Robert Slater, will make one realize that many Jews have excelled in a wide range of sports, not only the well known ones in baseball (Sandy Koufax, Hank Greenberg, Shawn Green), football (Sid Luckman), swimming (Mark Spitz), Olympic ice skating (Sarah and Emily Hughes), but also golf, tennis, basketball, boxing, track, gymnastics, and even ice hockey. In fact, in 2004 there were, according to Slater, five Jewish players in the NHL, Mathieu Schneider, Ron Stern, David Nemirovsky, Steve Dubinsky, and Doug Friedman. The number seems to be relatively constant; at the end of the 2013-14 season, the number remains at five, including Mike Brown, Mike Cammaleri, Jeff Halpern, Eric Nystrom and Trevor Smith.

Of course we should also mention the great Jewish coach, Red Auerbach, and sportscaster Howard Cosell. I'd like to relate stories of a few of these great men and women.

I'm sure that many of you know about Sandy Koufax, star pitcher for the Dodgers, who refused to pitch in the opening game of the 1965 World Series, which fell on Yom Kippur. What you may not know, but we find in Slater's biography of Koufax, is that the Dodgers lost that game, and the next day in the "St. Paul Pioneer Press" an editorial entitled "An Open Letter to Sandy Koufax" concluded with "The Twins love matza balls on Thursdays.". However, the Dodgers had the final word, when Koufax pitched the seventh game. The Dodgers won both the game and the World Series.

Slater has included a biography of a great Israeli track and field athlete, Esther Roth. Esther was a member of the 1972 Israeli Olympic track and field team. The Arab terrorist attack on the Israeli team (in Munich) resulted in the deaths of 11 of the Israeli athletes. Esther, a survivor, left the competition. In 1976 she returned to the Olympics, this time in Montreal, becoming the first Israeli athlete to reach the finals in an Olympic event, the 100-meter hurdles.

In an article in the Forward, October 7, 2005, Jewish sportswriter Gerald Eskenazi writes about ice hockey player Larry Zeidel, who played for the Philadelphia Flyers in the 1960's. Eskenazi tells this story:

In a game against the Boston Bruins, someone from the Bruins bench yelled, "You're next for the ovens, Zeidel!". That prompted some more fighting from Zeidel. Eskenazi continues, When I asked the president of the NHL, Clarence Campbell — who, as a Canadian lawyer, had worked on the Nuremburg war crimes tribunal — about what the Bruins had shouted, he told me, "The ethnic slur has always been part of hockey." No discipline was forthcoming against Boston just for that. Sports challenges us players to consider Torah injunctions. In last week's parasha, *Kedoshim,* in the same verse as the famous "Golden Rule," Leviticus 19:18, it is also written, "You shall not take vengeance or bear a grudge." In sports, retaliation for offenses real or perceived, whether punished or unpunished, is all too common. There is a widely held belief that if the referee allows it, it is OK. As a soccer referee for eight years, I ran across this often. But it is most assuredly not OK: the Torah forbids it.

In "The Midrash Says," edited by Rabbi Moshe Weissman, we find this definition: "Vengeance, then, is the act of requital to another according to his deeds, to do to him as he did to us, to repay him with evil if he did evil. This is forbidden by the Torah."

Now, in my eight years of soccer refereeing, one very unpleasant incident stands out. As I moved up the ranks, I began to get assignments to college soccer matches in the Western Washington region. At one such, I was working as one of the two linesmen, with a very experienced referee. The first half had the usual share of foul play. At halftime, we three officials walked off the field for a five-minute break, and the referee advised us to watch carefully one of the teams, because they believed in "the Israeli eye for an eye". I said nothing at the time, but later that night after arriving home, I called the referee assigner and complained about the incident, saying that I expected more professional behavior from referees, and that I would not work with this referee again unless he changed his attitude. I never again was called for any college soccer matches. Soon after that I quit soccer refereeing and went back to playing ice hockey. Which brings us back to *parashat Emor.* The part I did not mention at the beginning is at the end, where we find (Leviticus 24:17–20) one of the three places in the

Torah where the notorious "eye for an eye" passage appears. The others are Exodus 21:22–25 and Deuteronomy 19:21. In our *parasha,* we read, "One who kills a beast shall make restitution for it: life for life. If anyone maims his fellow, as he has done, so shall it be done to him: fracture for fracture, eye for eye, tooth for tooth."

In all cases, the commentaries from the Sages on to modern times say this means monetary compensation, not retaliation. Rashi says, "Our Rabbis explained that this does not mean placing an actual blemish on him, but rather the payment of money… therefore "giving" is written regarding it — something which is given from hand to hand."

Nechama Leibowitz, in "Studies in Vayikra," on *parashat Emor,* gives a very thorough discussion of the arguments of the Sages. In summary, they include: it cannot be implemented literally in practice, as in the case where the offender may be blind, and blind the victim (Rabbi Shimon bar Yochai), or in the case where blinding someone might result in his death (school of Hezekiah). Saddia Gaon argues on the basis of Samson's action against the Philistines, when Samson said, "As they did to me so I did to them," but what Samson did was not the same as what was done to him, so it should not be interpreted literally.

Finally, interpreting this injunction as a call for compensation is required in order to make it consistent with the law forbidding vengeance, which would be a literal interpretation of "eye for eye".

In "The Torah: A Modern Commentary," we find this footnote on our verse in *parashat Emor:* "There is no record of a single instance where a Jewish court carried out such retaliation; and Jewish tradition all but unanimously understood the language as referring to financial compensation."

Despite these facts, this "eye for an eye" passage has been used for centuries to slander the Torah, Judaism and the Jewish people. It still goes on today. I still hear from otherwise educated and thoughtful people that the God of the Old Testament (and Leviticus in particular) is a harsh and vengeful god. I take the time to explain Jewish views to them, if they are willing to listen. The struggle against ignorance is one of the most important ones we can take on, to make ourselves less ignorant and to study with others as well.

Thus, I would like to conclude by thanking Rabbi Borodin, the leaders of Congregation Beth Shalom and all the teachers who work so hard to help us learn Torah and apply it to make the world a better place.

A Brief Update

More recently, it seems, the ethnic slur is no longer part of ice hockey. In the second round of the 2014 Stanley Cup playoffs, the Montreal Canadiens (the "Habs," see "Who Were the Tishbites") won the first game of the NHL Eastern Conference semifinal series against the Boston Bruins. Montreal defenseman P.K. Subban scored the first goal against the Bruins as well as the winning goal in overtime. Subsequently, the Boston Bruins team announced their collective condemnation of the flurry of racist comments against Subban that circulated on various social media. The fans may not be much better, but the players speak for themselves. Progress is slow but should be celebrated.

Dialogue Between Friends

A friend had a series of frustrating and hurtful experiences at work. She came to me for advice, since I knew the context, and we had already had some conversations about the Jewish tradition and her experience in a Christian context. Here is her story.

I appreciate your advice. I will do my best to forgive Mr. D. for knocking me and my team to the ground on a few occasions. I will try to let go of attempting to understand the motivation and let go of the personal grudge. I will not embrace him but will let things be and get on with my task at hand.

Leviticus portrays a very stern and proscriptive God. I see irony here. T.

My reply:

Dear T.,

You don't need to forgive anyone. That is a separate matter from revenge or holding a grudge.

It seems to me that the statement: "Leviticus portrays a very stern and proscriptive God." comes from a Christian (and often negative) interpretation. A Jewish reading through the commentaries of the Sages (many of whom were contemporary with Jesus) presents exactly the opposite view.

It might be said that Leviticus (true to its Latin name, not its Hebrew name, *"Vayikra,"* meaning "He called") is very legalistic. Indeed it contains most of the legislation for the Israelite nation. So would you read the Congressional Record and say, "The US Laws portray a very stern and proscriptive government?" The statement takes legislation out of context.

What do you say of a set of laws that forbid cheating, forbid false testimony, provide legal rights for women and servants in a context where previously they had none, as well as many other ethical laws we take for granted today? Reread Leviticus. The same verse (19:18) that says, "You shall not seek revenge nor bear any grudge" finishes with "You shall love your neighbor as yourself" (the Sages interpreted "neighbor" very broadly, by the way). Jesus did not invent this idea. It was in Leviticus over a thousand years earlier. The Torah also gives rights to resident aliens, calls for caring for the stranger, the widow and the orphan, and lots more.

I'm doing a commentary at my synagogue on Saturday morning on the "eye for an eye" passage a little later in Leviticus. It is the most widely misinterpreted verse in the Bible. It has been used for millennia to slander the Jewish Bible and the Jews. The Sages said that this and the verses around it have to mean that when one person injures another the injured person is entitled to compensation for the value of the damage. They argued this logically and persuasively. It relates to the "Don't seek revenge or hold a grudge" verse, which makes the naive interpretation wrong.

Some crimes are capital crimes as specified in the Torah. So, don't we have such today? The difference is that no one in ancient Israel was ever actually executed. The Sages required such stringent tests of the reliability of witnesses and the nature of proof that it was not possible to effect this punishment. On the other hand, we live today in a society which not only legislates capital crimes, we really do execute people.

So, through Jewish eyes, there is no irony. I'm giving you the whole picture not the desiccated view that so many people are taught.

There is also a lot of stuff about the priests and ritual offerings but that is no longer applicable. Even that is radical in its time, as it replaced child sacrifice, found in other religious communities.

I'd be very interested in your reaction on taking another look at the actual text. Having said all that, forgiving people is good too. You are a wonderful per- son, and you make the time I spend with you worthwhile, including the time I've taken to write all this commentary.

Ira

Her response:

"You have me in a spin... a good one. My experience with organized religion has been less than helpful throughout my 48 years on this planet. My family has been a mix of zealots and those who have tried, and try, to live their lives in a way that is respectful of all and protective of their own... including the four-legged mammals and all other living things. I perceive that this is not far from the Jewish principle you want me to see in Leviticus from what I can determine. Living justly and in harmony with everyone else in my world is very important and a constant source of sadness... it is so hard to achieve. I bring so much pain on myself but our world is also a cauldron of pain and misery that my paltry little life has little impact on. I can't even figure out how to find peace in the workplace... not for a lack of trying. I am not ignorant either. I see the pitfalls and damage... I know how I contribute to the turmoil. I just don't know what I can do to make it better... not for myself alone but for all of us. Well that isn't totally true. I can change my heart. I just have to let go of any expectations that it makes a whit of difference. I had a call from a colleague today that was full of disparaging comments about individuals in our department... some things were said yesterday that put me and my team in a bad light. I wasn't there... should I react, hold a grudge or seek revenge for the misinformation that was given in a public forum? If I change something about myself and the way I interact will it have much impact beyond my own self-indulgence? It shouldn't be about my ego. If others perceive me in a bad light what should I do if my behavior and intent is true to the rule... or, for that matter, the word of God as set forth in Leviticus?

Some of the discourse I have read regarding Leviticus, I am sticking to the Jewish interpretations, show me a varied stance. One Rabbi was very much on the mark with what I think you are saying to me. Revenge and grudges are not acceptable but rebuke of wrongdoing is not a sin if one approaches the perceived wrongdoer as an equal in the eyes of God. Another Rabbi states that one must forgive and forget wrongdoing in order to eradicate grudges and the desire for revenge from your heart. Question... should the Jews forgive and forget the Holocaust? The Rabbi that spoke of being honorable in confronting the wrongdoer spoke of the destruction of the Temple and how it was brought forth by the inability of the people to face and confront the injustices brought upon them.

Our discourse of late caused me to pull out a letter that I sent to a Lutheran pastor who facilitated my cousin Michael's funeral in 1998. Michael died of massive heart failure at the age of 44 and left behind a devoted wife and three small children. The church was overflowing with community members who were touched by Michael. The pastor didn't know him but had some information, obviously, that did not put my cousin in good stead with the Lutheran community. His sermon was devastating to my family and to Michael's wife and children...

I am still grappling with this. The pastor did not respond to the letter that I sent to him. I quoted Matthew, "A good man out of the good treasure of the heart bringeth forth good things... and an evil man out of the evil treasure bringeth forth evil things. But I say unto you, that every idle word that men shall speak, they shall give account thereof on the day of judgement. For by thy words thou shall be justified... and by thy words thou shall be condemned." (Matthew 12:5,36,37) I shouldn't have taken this liberty with this man, to a point. I am not a biblical scholar like the pastor but I could not stop myself. So many people were hurt by this event. This episode comes to light for me because I sent the letter to this individual seeking revenge and I was holding a grudge in my heart. My family was hurting though… I was not alone in communicating our pain to this man of God. I am not even sure at this point that Matthew had it right. Judgement day is today and tomorrow, not necessarily the hereafter. Nobody has the right to assign eternal damnation to anyone. What about the here and now?

My family stopped attending this congregation after this. My cousin Kathy, Michael's sister, has been in spiritual pain for the last eight years due to this travesty. What to do?"

Respectfully yours, T.

Here is my reply:

Dear T.,

I have to admit that a lot of the questions you ask are beyond me. I'll just give a try at sharing some ideas.

Slander is very strictly forbidden in the Torah. The Sages say it was because of slander that the Temple was destroyed. (Your source is also correct the Sages gave many reasons.) You are right that rebuke of someone who commits serious offenses is also a commandment and it is not considered either revenge or bearing a grudge. We are not required to be accepting of abuse against us anymore than we should accept it being done to others. So it seems it would be a good idea to correct the misinformation and slander, and serve notice that it will not be tolerated. That is NOT revenge or grudge. The person who refused to lend his hammer did not commit any offense, but the slanderer violates the law. This is a tough distinction for many, but an important one. The Torah is not so demanding as people think — it asks that people just treat each other with respect, not that we be "saintly" beings. "Turn the other cheek" is not a Jewish idea.

The question about the Holocaust is well beyond my comprehension. Certainly we must not forget. If we forget, it will be repeated. Forgiving is another thing. I don't know what to do about that.

On "remediation every Sunday"— I guess I have a superficial understanding of this, but not an appreciation of the depth — the first part of Leviticus has all this stuff about the offerings. They were, I think, an early attempt to deal with and accept the fact that we are not perfect in our behavior, and need way to acknowledge it and then let go of it. It can be an experience of a compassionate God that forgives iniquity and sin (Exodus 34:6 – just after the Golden Calf episode).

Yes, Judaism is primarily focused on the here and now. It matters what we do. Here's a quote I like, from *Pirke Avot* (Sayings of the Fathers), chapter 4, verse 22, "Rabbi Yaakov… used to say, 'Better one hour of repentance and good deeds in this world than the entire life of the World to Come.'" Also in Pirke Avot, "The reward of a good deed is a good deed."

Your letter to the pastor sounds like a proper rebuke, not revenge.

As for my time, I like these discussions, and even better in person. You reward me with the fact that you care about this stuff. So do I.

Best wishes, Ira

Cancer and Torah

D'var Torah
Shabbat B'ha-alot'kha, 5768 (June 14, 2008)
Congregation Beth Shalom
Seattle, Washington

At Congregation Beth Shalom in Seattle, one Shabbat was chosen for special programming in addition to the regular service, as a "cancer survivors and caregivers Shabbat. "The organizers and participants in the liturgy that day are all members of this club that no one really wants to join. I had the privilege of being the guest *Darshan* that morning.

These words are dedicated to the memory of my friend, Lynn Mandel, and my student, Damian Potts, who both lived with love and courage to the very end, and left us way too soon.

The theme for today comes from the end of parasha *B'ha-alot'kha,* when Miriam is afflicted and Moses makes his famous passionate appeal on her behalf. It comes up in the Talmud in the context of the length of the prayer service. Here is the story, from *Tractate Brachot,* 34a, Soncino Edition:

Our Rabbis taught: Once a certain disciple went down before the Ark in the presence of Rabbi Eliezer, and he span out the prayer to a great length.

Rabbi Eliezer's disciples said to him: Master, how long-winded this fellow is! He replied to them: Is he drawing it out any more than our Master Moses, of whom it is written: The forty days and the forty nights? Another time it happened that a certain disciple went down before the Ark in the presence of Rabbi Eliezer and he cut the prayer very short. His disciples said to him: How concise this fellow is! Rabbi Eliezer replied to them: Is he any more concise than our Master Moses, who prayed, as it is written: Heal her now, O God, I beseech Thee? I will try to be reasonably concise. *B'ha-alot'kha* is filled with interesting instructions and narrative, starting with the menorah, then the purification of the Levites, the second Passover, the cloud over the Tabernacle, the trumpets and the march, the plea for meat, and finally, the incident of Miriam and Aaron's criticism of Moses. One interesting thing to note is that in this *parasha,* verses 10:35 and 10:36 (page 826 of *Etz Hayim*), form a frame for the Torah Service. We sing verse 35, *"vay'hi binsoa ha-aron,"* when we take the Torah out, and we say silently verse 36, *"u'v'nucho yomar,"* when we return it to the ark. So, in the Torah Service we reenact the procession through the wilderness.

However, what I want to concentrate on first is the name of the *parasha,* B'ha-alot'kha, which is about the lighting of the menorah. Our *chumash* translates this as "mount," perhaps referring to the lifting up of the menorah to its place or the ascent of the priest on a platform to reach the lamps. This is consistent with the *shoresh, ayin-lamed-hey,* which has the meaning of lifting up or going up. However, others translate this as "light" or "kindle," since the same word is used in *parasha Tetzaveh*, referring to the *Ner Tamid* (*Etz Hayim*, page 503). There it clearly means to "kindle" the regular light. This raised the question of why the verb *l'ha-alot* is used instead of the more direct, *l'hadlik*, as in the blessing for kindling lights.

Rashi offers several explanations. First, Rashi writes, "because the flame rises, igniting is described in terms of rising." He further observes that it is necessary to persist in the ignition process until the flame becomes self-sufficient, i.e., fully lit. Here he cites the *Gemara*, Shabbat 21a, "the flame must ascend of itself and not through something else." Rashi's third explanation is that the Menorah was on a tall lampstand, and it was necessary for the *kohein* to ascend a platform to be able to reach the lamps from above.

In English we have the expression "to bring up the lights" (in the theater), referring to the gradual raising of the lights to their full brightness. We also speak of "raising children." More about that in a moment.

The Hebrew word for elevator is *ma-alit,* plural *ma-aliyot.* This translates into English as "lift". The sense of lifting also in English is rendered as "to carry" or "to bear". Thus, in a hotel in a non-English speaking country, one day the elevators were not working, so the hotel staff put out a sign saying, "The management regrets that you will be unbearable today."

Of course we are familiar with the idea of *aliyah,* going up for the honor of blessings before and after the Torah reading. The same word is used to refer to going to Israel to live.

Now, that leads us to a more metaphorical sense of *l'ha-alot,* which is eloquently expressed by the Lubavitcher Rebbe, Rabbi Menachem Mendel Schneerson, in his book, *Torah Studies.* He notes that in Proverbs, 20:27, it is written, "The lamp of HaShem is the soul of humankind." Thus, he says, "the lamps of the Menorah of the Sanctuary are a symbol of the Jewish soul." The job of lighting applies to kindling the flame in our souls, not just to start, but to persist until each of us can give light by ourselves. Thus, the job of raising children has as its goal to teach and help them so that they can eventually take care of themselves.

So, what has this got to do with cancer? Those who are afflicted are souls that need lifting up. Caregivers are those whose job is like that of the priests, to light the lamps of the afflicted. Taking care of those struggling with cancer takes persistence, to help them to fully realize their potential. And, just as the priests needed to ascend to be able to light the Menorah, the caregivers must "rise to the occasion," to gather the strength for this huge task.

Who are the afflicted and who are the caregivers? The simple answer is that the afflicted are those who have been diagnosed with cancer, and the caregivers are those who provide for them sustenance and friendship, medical aid, and so on.

Another answer is that those who are related to the person with cancer are afflicted because they see their loved one facing adversity and it tears their hearts. Those with cancer then become the caregivers, because we are challenged to be there for our loved ones, despite our disease. Ultimately, we all must support and lift up each other, because the burden of being a caretaker can (and often does) become unbearable, as does the struggle with cancer itself.

Now, we skip to the end of our *parasha,* to Miriam. What happened here?

Miriam says something slanderous about Moses. God punishes Miriam with an affliction. Moses, who should be offended, intercedes and pleads with God to heal her. What's wrong with this story?

First, do the wicked really get punished and the righteous rewarded? Is skin disease a sign that a person has sinned? Indeed our literary tradition is filled with such statements. My father, Binyamin ben David v'Shoshana, would have called this "superstitious hooey". People do not get cancer because God is punishing them for something they did wrong. The world that God created is marvelous, and full of possibilities. It allows for things to happen that make pain for us, and it allows for this to happen independently of anything we do. It also allows for great beauty and for wonderful things to happen. It follows natural laws, only a small part of which we understand. Some of that understanding gives us some options. We can in many cases successfully treat some cancers, and we can change some things in our world so as to prevent or reduce the incidence of cancer. But it is never useful to indulge in guilt feelings.

Second, for what do we pray? We, like Moses, pray for healing for those who are ill. Do we expect God to actually and personally intercede? I don't. My prayer is an expression of my feelings of love for my family and my friends, my fear for what is happening to some of them, my wish that things would get better. We need this outpouring. It gives us affirmation for our caring. It can give us strength, to do our part in caregiving. For those of us who also pray for ourselves, it gives us the courage and determination to face the next treatment, the next phase of challenges, which surely will be coming. Prayer brings us together so that we can support each other, and lift ourselves and each other.

So, I hope that I will have the privilege of standing here two years from now, to again share words of Torah with you all. I would like to thank you for all that you have done for me, to lift me up and to care for me as I have been going through my own confrontation with metastatic kidney cancer. And I pray that we all have the strength to keep the lifts working, that we may all be bearable, today and each day.

An Awe-inspiring Yom Kippur,

D'var Torah
Fall 5770, (2009)
Congregation Beth Shalom
Seattle, Washington

Sometimes on Shabbat or holidays, in addition to the d'var Torah which usually follows the Torah reading, a brief introduction to the main themes or events of the reading is provided. Here is one for Yom Kippur.

Thanks to Rabbi Borodin for honoring me with the request to introduce the Torah reading for Yom Kippur morning. I confess to being a little nervous about this awesome task, on this awesome day, as we contemplate what may be in store for us in the new year. The Torah reading for Yom Kippur morning is from Parashat Acharei Mot, together with a special maftir, from Parashat Pinchas, that details the practices and offerings for Yom Kippur. The passage from Acharei Mot focuses on the job of the Kohen Gadol, or High Priest, to prepare the sanctuary and conduct the rituals that will atone for the sins of all of Israel. The process is complex, and has many nuances worthy of study, such as the order in which he prepares the incense, and brings the offering. It also has a unique part, found nowhere else, that of the two goats. Aaron is instructed to cast lots, so that one goat will be sacrificed in much the manner of other offerings, while the other will be kept alive for a very strange process. Aaron is to lay hands on the head of the goat, confessing all the sins of Israel, thus transferring them to the goat.

Then, another individual is assigned to take the goat into the wilderness, to Azazel. The final fate of the goat is not specified in the Torah, but the Mishnah (Yoma 6:6) suggests that the goat was sent over a cliff, taking the sins of Israel with it to its death.

The necessity of some kind of ritual by which we express our repentance, and what that ritual should be, are challenging questions. In our time, in the absence of the Temple and the Kohen Gadol, the ritual described in the Torah is not performed, though it is commemorated in a special section of the Musaf service of Yom Kippur. In general, we have inherited prayer as a replacement for the sacrifice system, though even the nature of the prayers in some cases has evolved somewhat away from specific recollection of the details of the sacrifices. Vestiges or offshoots such as Kapparot remain in some parts of the Jewish community, and are much debated. The ritual of our Torah portion gives us the term "scapegoat," which does not carry a very positive or uplifting meaning. Yet, it is not possible to live without some way of atoning for the mistakes all of us have made and will make. The prospect of not being forgiven, or not being able to forgive ourselves, is terrifying.

Regarding my anxiety today, I would like to tell you about something that happened a few weeks ago. On the Shabbat before Rosh HaShanah, I was here with my granddaughter Morrigan (then 7 years old). Jackie Bayley kindly offered me the seventh aliyah. I told Morrigan we would be going up to the bimah shortly. She told me she was really scared. She clutched my arm and said, "I'm going to hold onto you for dear life." I reassured her and all went well. It reminded me of the passage from Proverbs (3:18) that concludes our Torah service, "It is a tree of life to those who hold fast to it..." So, we will now read from our Torah, we will learn with Rabbi Borodin, and, as we move through this long day, we will hold on for dear life.

What's in a Name?

D'var Torah
Shabbat Sh'mot, 5772 (January 14, 2012)
Congregation Beth Shalom
Seattle, Washington

The second book of the Torah is known in English as "Exodus" because of the centrality of that narrative. Its Hebrew name, *Sh'mot,* however, comes from the first significant word of the first weekly portion. The Hebrew word means in English simply, "Names."

This week's *parasha, Sh'mot,* is aptly named. These first chapters are, in modern terms, action packed with many heroic and interesting characters. It is too much for a short morning commentary, so I will concentrate on only one element, the idea of a name.

The very first verse begins by saying, "These are the names of the sons of Israel who came to Egypt with Jacob, each coming with his household." Already we see the multiplicity of meaning that can be associated with a name. Here, our *Chumash* says, "Israel" refers to Jacob, but just as Jacob was transformed by an encounter with an angel, his descendants will be transformed by a collective encounter with God.

A count is given, "The total number... came to seventy, Joseph being already in Egypt." (The Hebrew simply reads, "and Joseph was in Egypt.") So why was Joseph mentioned here specifically? Rashi gives a dual reason,

"...to let you know how righteous Joseph was — the same Joseph who tended his father's sheep, is the same Joseph who was in Egypt and he became king, yet he remained in his righteousness." The traditional emphasis is that Joseph remained true to his tradition and connection with his family despite being in a foreign land. However, there is the very difficult matter of verifying that these are the same person. Earlier in the Torah (Genesis 45:3–13), when Joseph finally revealed himself to his brothers, he took some measures to convince his brothers that indeed it was him. In modern times, we have this problem every day. Many of our interactions with commercial, social and government institutions require that we identify ourselves as the same individuals that these institutions have on record. When I call my Internet Service Provider or bank, or the medical center where I am a patient, it is not enough to give my name; I have to answer a series of questions about me. These, more than a password or patient account number, serve to give the other person confidence that I am who I say I am. Thus, identity management in our time is not so different from antiquity.

The idea that each of us is an individual with a unique identity, even if we share the same names, is central to the Torah and to life. It is recognized in a wonderful passage in the Talmud, Sanhedrin 17a, in the Mishnah that talks about the requirements for witnesses in capital cases:

[Man was created singly] to proclaim the greatness of the Holy One, Blessed be He: for if a man strikes many coins from one mold, they all resemble one another, but the Supreme King of Kings, the Holy One, Blessed be He, fashioned every man in the stamp of the first man, and yet not one of them resembles his fellow. Therefore every single person is obliged to say: 'The world was created for my sake'.

This is the miracle we now understand as the Genetic Code, DNA and the mechanisms of reproduction and mutation. Identity plays out in a very different way in the realm of physics. Every electron behaves in an identical way to every other electron, and moreover, they are indistinguishable in a way that gives rise to the entire world. It seems that there is an exclusion principle, articulated by the famous Swiss Jewish physicist, Wolfgang Pauli, that no two electrons can be in exactly the same state. Without this, there would be no atoms, no molecules, no life and nothing interesting going on in the Universe. This was a source of wonderment for Princeton University graduate student Richard Feynman and his adviser, Professor John Wheeler. One night Wheeler called Feynman and excitedly stated, "Feynman, I know why all the electrons behave in exactly the same way. It's because they are all the same electron." The idea did not hold up, but led to another remarkable idea, that eventually revolutionized theoretical physics, and for which Feynman later shared the Nobel Prize in 1965 with two other brilliant physicists, Julian Schwinger and Sin-Itiro Tomonaga. If you will indulge me I'll share with you a little more about names in mathematics and science. In mathematics, names are temporary ways to refer to things, and have no intrinsic meaning. The letters in algebraic equations can be operated on to solve the equations. In school, children learn this idea of abstraction by solving so-called "story problems," in which a cast of abstract characters is said to participate in some activity that can be represented by mathematical equations. This is how physics works. We make up names for things like the properties of electrons and then we put the names into equations and solve them. The frustration of children with this lack of meaning for names must be familiar to everyone. Some time ago, the Canadian humorist, Stephen Leacock, wrote about the mythic characters, who appear in the story problems. His essay is called, "A, B and C, the Human Element in Mathematics." It is reprinted in an anthology by Clifton Fadiman, "The Mathematical Magpie" and can also be found on the Internet with most any web search engine.

But I digress. Back to the Torah. There is in *parashat Sh'mot* another aspect of names a scientist, to be curious and observe. What happens next is a recurring motif. Chapter 3, verse 4 says, "God called to him out of the bush: 'Moses! Moses!'" The response from Moses is a dramatic shift in orientation, as he responds, *"Hineni,"* or "Here I am." Moses the observer shifts to Moses in a relationship with God. Martin Buber's work, "I and Thou," expounds this in the context of attempting to understand identity and relationship as intimately connected. The I-it relationship is one in which we can observe, catalog, describe and yet be apart from that which is observed. The I-Thou relationship is an engagement with the other. We do both and need both, and find our identity in the union of the two. But while the I-it relationship is necessary, the I-Thou relationship is paramount. Buber succinctly states, "All real living is meeting."

God asks Moses to speak to the Israelites and to Pharaoh. Moses needs to know what to say when they ask about God, "What is His name?" God's response, verse 14, has puzzled generations,

And God said to Moses, *"Ehyeh–Asher–Ehyeh"*. He continued, "Thus shall you say to the Israelites, '*Ehyeh* sent me to you.'" The Hebrew translates word for word as "I will be what I will be." Our *Chumash, Eitz Chaim,* notes that the phrase has been variously interpreted, "I am whatever I choose to be" (this is echoed in the end of the Book of Job), "I am pure becoming," and other elaborations. We learn that naming God or describing God does not succeed. One of the first things you find in a stage play is a list of the cast of characters, by name and description. So, too, with the Talmud, and with all the tradition from Sinai to now, we relate to the great scholars by learning their names and engaging with their words and ideas. It struck me as curious, then, that there is one, an early Amora, who is known only by the title, "Rav," the Great One. The Steinsaltz English Talmud Reference Guide notes that his actual name was "Abba Arikha" and that he was the founder of the great academy of Sura in Babylonia.

We have today a famous sports figure who similarly is known simply as "The Great One". Perhaps someone here knows the actual name of this individual? I'll hint that the sport in which he excelled is near and dear to me.

I have another personal connection with Rav. Terry, my wife, has done a lot of genealogy research and was able to trace back many centuries in her family tree. One night I was looking over her shoulder at the family tree display and saw the name "Natronai." I asked her if she knew who this was. She said, no, it just turned up as she went through various links and sources. I said I thought it would be Natronai ben Nehemiah, the Gaon of Pumbedita, the other great academy of Babylonia. More recently I learned that there is another Natronai, Natronai ben Hilai, who was the Gaon of Sura in a different century. Terry is still working on this to determine which one might indeed be her ancestor. I am so honored to be married to a descendant of a great Jewish scholar.

As much fun as it is, we now leave genealogy and pick up the thread of earlier, the lingering question posed by Moses, "[when] they ask me 'What is His name?' what shall I say to them?" In "The Torah: A Modern Commentary," edited by Gunther Plaut (also known as the Plaut Chumash), it is noted that Moses is likely asking for himself, since he never reuses the answer.

Moses wants to know the nature of God by inquiring about the inner meaning of His name, but God will not be fully known and therefore evades a clear answer. Later in the Torah (Ki Tissa, Exodus 33:18 and following), Moses tries another approach, asking to see God's face, and God answers, I will make all My goodness pass before you, and I will proclaim before you the name *Adonoy,* and the grace that I grant and the compassion that I show. But you cannot see My face, for man may not see Me and live.

Even for myself, I cannot come up with an adequate answer to the ultimate question "Who are you?" The process of relationship seems to be the only grasp we have on an answer. And the study of Torah is our grasp for an answer to the question of Moses, as expressed in the Introduction in the *Plaut Chu-mash,* "The Torah is Israel's distinctive record of its search for God." May we continue the search with joy and love.

Imagination

The D'var Torah
Shabbat Balak, 5773 (June 22, 2013)
Congregation Beth Shalom
Seattle, Washington

Parashat Balak is unusual in that it is said to contain "what may be the only comic passage in the Torah." (Etz Hayim, page 894). The stage has been set in the previous *parasha*, when Balak, King of Moab, refuses to allow the Israelites passage through Moab. Moses leads the people on an alternate route, where they encounter hardships and battles, and eventually turn again to traverse the land of Moab. Now Balak has a problem. Israel has been successful in battle and is coming his way. He sends for Baalam, known as the greatest prophet among the non-Jews, asking him to curse the Israelites, hoping this will help him prevail. God says to Baalam, "Don't go" and Baalam indeed refuses the assignment. Balak further entreats, and this time God says he may go but will be constrained to say only what words He puts in Baalam's mouth.

Baalam sets out on his donkey, but on the path an angel blocks the way. The donkey can see the angel but Baalam cannot. Three times the donkey refuses to move forward and three times Baalam beats the donkey. Finally the donkey speaks. "What have I done to you that you have beaten me these three times?" (Numbers 22:28) to which Baalam responds, "You have made a mockery of me!" The donkey answers by asking rhetorically (verse 30), "Look, I am the ass that you have been riding all along until this day!

135

Have I been in the habit of doing thus to you?" to which Baalam answers, "No." Then Baalam is able to see the angel, and is scolded by God. Baalam is allowed to proceed, and meets Balak, but cautions Balak that he can only say what God dictates to him. He (Baalam) then spoke three times, each time reciting a short poem, in effect blessing, not cursing, the Israelites. The third of these begins with the pronouncement we know so well and recite as we enter the synagogue, and begin the morning prayers.

Mah Tovu "How goodly are your tents, O Jacob, your dwelling places O Israel." This story raises many questions. Did God really speak to Baalam, or was it a dream? Was there really an angel? Did the donkey really speak? The story blurs the boundaries between the world of our direct experiences and the world of our imagination. Does such a world exist?

My favorite Shakespeare play, "A Midsummer Night's Dream," develops an entertaining and provocative tale with this blurring of boundaries as its central theme. It is a tale of interaction between the world of people and the world of fairies, of magical things happening, of a play within a play, put on by the workmen of Athens, in which, during a rehearsal, the fairies turn the head of the lead player (whose name is "Bottom") into the head of an ass. The next day, after all is set right once again, the workmen assemble to put on their play for Theseus, the Duke of Athens and his bride to be, Hippolyta, Queen of the Amazons. The Duke comments on the strange tales of the happenings of the night before (Act V, Scene I):

Hippolyta: 'Tis strange, my Theseus, that these lovers speak of.'Theseus: 'More strange than true... The lunatic, the lover and the poet Are of imagination all compact. One sees more devils than vast Hell can hold, that is the madman. The lover, all as frantic, Sees Helen's beauty in a brow of Egypt and as the Duke continues, in his voice we hear Shakespeare's comment on the creative process, The poet's eye in a fine frenzy rolling,' Doth glance from heaven to earth, from earth to heaven, And as imagination bodies forth The forms of things unknown, the poet's pen Turns them to shapes, and gives to airy nothing A local habitation and a name.'

Imagination is essential to the story of Baalam, and to the poems he recites. We will come back to this shortly. For a few moments I turn to the world of science, to tell two personal stories.

When I was in high school I had the opportunity to spend a Summer working in a physical chemistry research laboratory at the Polytechnic Institute of Brooklyn. This program was sponsored by the US National Science Foundation (NSF). So it was, that part way through the Summer a staff member of the NSF came by the laboratory to meet with me (and the other students in the program) to see how we were doing. Among other things he asked me what I thought were important qualities a scientist should have in order to be successful. I said I imagined it would be important to be very skilled in mathematics, or at least be a strong logical thinker. He said, "Yes, that's good, but what else?" So, I said I imagined it would be important to work hard and not be easily discouraged. Again he replied, "Yes, that's good too, but what else?" Thinking as hard as I could, I said I imagined it would be important to be able to work with others in a team. Somehow I still had not hit on what he had in mind, so I asked him. He said, "Well, you actually mentioned it three times. To be a scientist you have to have a lot of imagination!"

He was so right. As I learned more about physics, I realized the things that physicists talk about have never really been seen, electrons, protons, quarks, the electromagnetic field, gravity, and so on. Like the poet, the scientist makes up names and describes relationships, thus giving to "airy nothing" something we can imagine and think about. We talk about radio waves and light waves, but what is waving? At first, physicists thought that space was filled with some substance they called the "Ether" but this was abandoned in favor of simply imagining something we call the "Electromagnetic field," described by mathematical symbols and equations.

My Ph.D. dissertation was called, "Low energy meson production by real and virtual photons." My Mom asked me what a photon was. I told her it is an elementary particle with no mass and no charge, that spins like a top. Then she asked, "What's a virtual photon?" I explained that it was one that could not be measured in an experiment, but only appeared in the formulas to be used in the calculations. So Mom decided that my research was about "Nothing that spins and does not really exist."

The equations of physics are actually poems written in a very arcane language, mathematics, that, unfortunately, few people understand.

Now back to Baalam. He could not imagine what was going on with the donkey, but instead got angry that the donkey did not do what he wanted. This contrasts with Moshe Rabbenu, who, when confronted with the burning bush, did not take it as an attempt by someone to trick him or bother him. Instead he approached it as a scientist, and investigated, observed, listened and used his imagination.

The Torah, not only in parashat Balak, but in many other ways, calls us to imagine that the world is something much more than what we see, that using imagination in the right way, we can live a deeply meaningful life.

So, I would like to invite you to exercise your imagination and share your thoughts about this question:

What might you do in a situation like that of Baalam and the donkey, where something is happening that may not be as it seems? Have you encountered something like that and how did it go? How does imagination help? Perhaps it can also hinder.

Finally, I would like to return to Baalam's third poem. What did he see, or imagine he saw, when he said, "How lovely are your tents, O Jacob..."? Rashi says, "Because he saw that their entrances were not facing each other." This is dealt with in the Talmud (Bava Batra 60a) where the question of openings between the courtyard and residences or between courtyards is discussed in relation to privacy.

However, there is another idea, supported by a midrash (Gen. Rabbah LXV. 20), cited in Cohen, "Everyman's Talmud" (pp. 173-4): No philosophers have arisen in the world like Balaam the son of Beor and Oenomaos of Gadara. All the heathens assembled to the latter and said to him, "Tell us how we may successfully contend against the people of Israel." He answered, "Go to their Synagogues and Schools, and if you hear there the clamor of children rehearsing their lessons, you cannot prevail against them; for so their patriarch (Isaac) assured them, saying 'The voice is the voice of Jacob and the hands are the hands of Esau' (Genesis 27:22), meaning that when Jacob's voice is heard in the House of Assembly, the hands of Esau are powerless."

So, we should imagine that Baalam saw in the tents the children and their teachers learning together. This is one of many sources that show how important education is considered by the Torah and our tradition more broadly. So, thanks to Rabbi Borodin and to you all for this opportunity to learn together. In so doing, we assure that we and our tradition will persist and thrive, through education.

High Drama

The D'var Torah
Shabbat Vayera, 5774 (December 28, 2013)
Congregation Beth Shalom,
Seattle, Washington

On Passover, the rabbis teach, we have two obligations: to eat only matzah (unleavened bread), and to tell the story of the Exodus from Egypt. The story has continued to be told for generations, indeed for millennia. It has been the basis for two very popular and successful feature films. This commentary suggests why it has been so captivating for so long.

You may remember a very popular folk song called "Where have all the flowers gone?" written by Pete Seeger and Joe Hickerson, and performed over the ensuing decades by many legendary singers and groups. The refrain echoes in my head to this day, and is a reflection of an aspect of this week's parasha, *Vayera*. *Parashat Vayera* continues the dramatic story of the confrontation between Moses and Pharaoh, relating the events of the first seven of the Ten Plagues.

IN the beginning of the *parasha*, the word vayera is translated as "I appeared." The root, however, has the meaning of "fear" or "awe". Thus, we could also read this as "I awed Abraham, Isaac and Jacob." Indeed the narrative in which God appears to each of the patriarchs is one of unusual events, designed to impress on them the significance of the revelation. But despite the drama, the generations of descendants of the patriarchs (and matriarchs) seem to forget, and to lose sight of their destiny and mission.

Moses addresses the Israelites to convey the promise of redemption, in verses 6-8, "I am the Lord, I will free you from the labors of the Egyptians, and deliver you from their bondage. I will redeem you with an outstretched arm and through extraordinary chastisements. And I will take you to be my people, and I will be your God. And you shall know that I, the Lord, am your God who freed you from the labors of the Egyptians."

The Israelites did not embrace this message. They had already seen the cruel response from Pharaoh in the first encounter (previously described in *parashat Sh'mot*). When God directs Moses again to go to Pharaoh, Moses says, "The Israelites would not listen to me; how then should Pharaoh heed me, a man of impeded speech!" But God reaffirms the directive to Moses, and adds that

God will "harden Pharaoh's heart, that I may multiply My signs and marvels in the land of Egypt."

In the high drama that follows, Moses and Aaron confront Pharaoh with plague after plague, blood, frogs, vermin, wild beasts, pestilence, boils and hail. Each time Pharaoh agrees to let the Israelites go, and when the plague is lifted he refuses to release the Israelites. The severity of the plagues escalates. Next week's *parasha, Bo,* relates the last three plagues, locusts, darkness, and finally the death of the first born, after which the Israelites are expelled from Egypt.

The story is so central to Jewish identity, to understanding Torah and living Judaism, that we are commanded to re-enact and retell it in the observance of Passover. But why is the extreme high drama necessary? The plain meaning, from the text itself, is that through the extraordinary nature of the plagues, the Israelites and the Egyptians will recognize that the God of the Israelites is the one God, the true and all powerful God. This is necessary for the Israelites to restore the faith they lost through centuries of oppression. The Israelites also become an agent through which God becomes known to all the world, as the beginning of the Haftarah, from Ezekiel, points out, "Thus said the Lord God: When I have gathered the House of Israel from the peoples among which they have been dispersed, and have shown Myself holy through them in the sight of the nations, they shall settle on their own soil..."

It seems that the impact will not last. At Mount Sinai, Moses goes up to receive the Torah, and as described in *parashat Ki Tisa*, the people become impatient and build a Golden Calf. Moses pleads on their behalf and after punishment and repentance, the journey continues.

This process of failure and rededication is a recurrent theme in the Biblical narrative. It is also reflected in the *haftarah* for *Ki Tisa*, from I Kings, which relates a later time when Ahab becomes the King of the northern kingdom of Israel, and again people return to idol worship. The prophet Elijah confronts the prophets of Ba'al before Ahab and the assembled people of Israel. But before the contest he addresses the Israelites (Verse 18:21): And Elijah drew near to all the people, and said, How long will you go limping between two opinions? If the Lord be God, follow Him; but if Ba'al, then follow him. And the people answered not a word.

My friend and teacher, Avi Ehrlich, explained that the word pesachim, translated here as "limping," is the same root as pesach, the Hebrew name for the holiday of Passover. This root indeed means, to skip, hop, or pass over. In its usage in *parashat Bo*, verses 12:11 and 12:13, describing how the Israelites will be spared in the final plague, God will "pass over" the marked Israelite households. However it requires that the Israelites duly mark their doorposts. They must not waver, but make clear which path they will follow.

Now, in the confrontation with Ahab, Elijah calls on the Israelites again to choose. It seems that a dramatic demonstration is again necessary. The prophets of Ba'al do their procedures and invoke their deity, but nothing happens. Elijah drenches the altar, the offering and the wood with water, and calls to God (verses 18:37-39), and this time the people respond:

Then the fire of the Lord fell, and consumed the burnt sacrifice, and the wood pile, and the stones, and the dust, and licked up the water that was in the trench. And when the people saw it, they fell on their faces; and they said, "The Lord, He is the God; the Lord, He is the God."

The cry of the people is the concluding line of the liturgy for Yom Kippur. The liturgy of Yom Kippur is intended to create a dramatic experience once again to evoke our choice to follow God.

We are not unique. Having facts and evidence before us, human beings in the broader community too are hard pressed to accept them and act appropriately. I will just mention an example from my profession of science in medicine. In the 1840s, in the dawn of modern medicine, maternity hospitals had a very high incidence rate of what was then known as "puerpural fever." Women admitted to maternity wards were contracting this disease and dying along with their babies. There were several accepted "explanations" for this disease.

There were some anomalies, noticed by a young Hungarian physician named Ignaz Semmelweis. He began a series of experiments to test these explanations, none of which were supported by any of his results. Then he discovered that whatever was causing this illness was being spread by medical students and physicians who came to obstetric exams from their instruction with cadavers, without washing their hands. He also demonstrated that infections were spread from one patient to another by the physicians, and that having the physicians wash their hands before and in between exams in a strong cleaning solution would drastically cut the rate of infection. He published his findings. The result was that he was ridiculed by the profession and fired from his job at the Vienna General Hospital. He became very disturbed and was committed to an asylum where he died shortly after admission. Later the work of Lister and Pasteur confirmed and further explained his findings. It was the beginning of our understanding of the germ theory of disease.

A few years ago, at a local university medical center where I worked (I am now retired), I noticed one day that all over the hospital, posters had gone up, with pictures of the medical director, nurses and other physicians, most of whom I knew. On each poster was printed, "My name is... (filled in). Ask me if I have washed my hands." So, 160 years after Semmelweis published evidence showing the importance of this procedure, my hospital was finally getting a campaign going to enforce it.

Also some years ago, I participated in a committee of the School of Medicine, one of whose objectives was to introduce the idea of Evidence Based Medicine in the curriculum. After listening a while and having a hard time following what they were saying, I asked if someone would explain what is Evidence Based Medicine. They said, it is where clinical care is guided by the best scientific evidence. So, I asked, "Then, what have doctors been doing up until now?"

You can come up with many other examples from all areas of modern life. It seems that we are not going to pay attention until something dramatic happens, some disaster or tragedy. And that ongoing inability to act until things get really terrible is the connection to the Pete Seeger song, in which each verse ends with the refrain,

"When will they ever learn? When will they ever learn?"

A Stamp of Approval

The next day I received a surprising and delightful email from Kevin Coskey, a friend and also a member of Congregation Beth Shalom:

Gail and I both appreciated your D'var Torah yesterday. I had heard the Semmelweis story before, but Gail had not. She read about him last night and discovered that many decades after his death, Hungary issued a postage stamp in his honor. This inspired her to look through her father's stamp collection. Indeed, she found the stamp, an image of which is attached.

Here it is, reprinted with permission from Gail Coskey.

Gail wrote a little more background: Kevin sent me a link from Wikipedia, (http://en.wikipedia.org/wiki/Ignaz_Semmelweis) which mentions a stamp of Semmelweis. I have my father's stamp collection. I was interested in stamps when I was little. I thought maybe he had the Semmelweis stamp in his collection since it was from 1937. (My dad was born in 1927.) I looked into Hungary pages and found it! I spent some time looking at all the stamps. I wish I had asked him where he got all of his stamps. I plan to show the stamps to my kids since there is so much history and stamps from countries that do not exist anymore or are called different names. I also mentioned your d'var to my brother who is an Infectious Disease doctor. He knew of him and said he was the father of [our understanding of] Infectious Disease.

What was the name of the book that is the fictional story of Semmelweis life? I thought that would make a good gift for him.

The book is called "The Cry and the Covenant," by Morton Thompson. It was first published in the 1940's, a hundred years after Semmelweis lived. In 1971 I was employed as a laboratory technician at the Harborview Microbiology Lab for the night shift (that was what an unemployed Ph.D. did in those days). The Director of the Laboratory, C. Evans Roberts, M.D., had put together a little library, including standard reference texts on microbiology. I found the book there, and read it during slow shifts when there was nothing else pending. It is still in print and available from a local bookstore.

Explanations

The D'var Torah
Shabbat Chukat, 5774 (June 28, 2014)
Congregation Beth Shalom
Seattle, Washington

Heidi Piel, Rabbi Borodin's assistant, wrote to me earlier this week to confirm, in her words, "that you are the purveyor of wisdom this coming Shabbat as the guest Darshan." I replied that indeed I would serve as the guest Darshan but could not guarantee that I would offer any wisdom. This is true as you will shortly see.

The Torah portion this week, *Chukat,* begins with a detailed set of instructions for the mitzvah concerning the "Red Heifer". The procedure is provided as a means of purification of those who become impure by coming into contact with a human corpse, for example at a burial or in preparation for a burial. Many other matters are related in our parasha, but this strange mitzvah will be our stepping off point.

The ritual contains several strange elements, that seem to demand explanation. Why does the mixture purify the person who has become impure? Why does the person sprinkling it, who starts out pure, become impure? What exactly is "purity?" Here are some thoughts of the Sages.

The Midrash says (Numbers Rabbah 19:8, as quoted in the *Plaut Chumash*, page 1149) that there are four mitzvot in the Torah that are unexplainable: the law requiring a man to marry his brother's widow, the law forbidding the mixing of wool and linen in one's garments, the law concerning the scapegoat (Azazel) and the law of the Red Cow.

Rashi says it cannot be given a reason and is therefore called a statute. He argues that Satan and the nations of the world will demand an explanation, thus the intent of the term "statute" is, "I have decreed it, and you are not permitted to question it." R. Menachem Mendel Schneerson, z"l, adds a clarification, based on the seeming redundancy of the use of both "statute" and "law". As noted, there are are other mitzvot that seem not to be completely explainable, but can have some partial explanation, while the strange rules of the purification ritual of the Red Cow cannot be explained at all. It is in a class by itself.

Finally, even the great King Solomon (Ecclesiastes 7:23) admits, "I said I will be wise; but it was far from me." and the Midrash (Numbers *Rabbah* 19:3, again, from the *Plaut Chumash*, page 1149) explains that this refers to Solomon's inability to discern the meaning or reason for the commandment concerning the Red Cow. So if these Sages say it is beyond explanation, I am not about to pretend I have some wisdom on this matter.

Instead, I will resort to a strategy that may still lead to something interesting. I would like to move up a level of thinking and talk about explanation itself. I'll start with physics, about which I do know something. Don't worry, ice hockey will get mentioned along the way, and finally we will return to Torah.

It seems that explanation is very difficult, whether we are seeking to understand the world, Torah, ourselves or other people. This was really made clear by an incident many years ago when my wife, Terry, was the Principal of the religious school at Temple B'nai Torah. When children were acting out in class we teachers would send them to Terry, who has amazing skill with managing young children. When a child arrived at Terry's office, she would ask them to explain to her what happened. One day Terry was sitting in the teacher's lounge (at the Jewish Day School where we rented space for the TBT school). The door was open. Two young boys were walking down the sidewalk. As they passed, Terry overheard one say to the other, "You better behave because if you don't you will have to explain yourself to Terry."

Scientists seek to create explanations of the complex and beautiful patterns and things we see in the world. Our approach to this is to imagine or guess some basic principles, from which we can then predict what we will observe or measure in an experiment. Sometimes the prediction involves many mathematical or logical calculations in order to get from the principles to the predictions. That is the theoretical side of physics. If the observations or measurements agree with the predictions, we accept the principles as valid.

It is of course important to check the calculations carefully to make sure you did not make a mistake, and it is equally important for the experimenters to check their work. Both the calculations and the measurements should give the same results regardless of who does them, if they have been careful about every step. Generally, we look for the most compact principles, the fewer the better. In the words of Albert Einstein, "The supreme task of the physicist is to arrive at those universal elementary laws from which the cosmos can be built up by pure deduction."

Thus we have the idea that the world is made up of atoms, of which there are some one hundred different kinds. But further simplification is possible. Each atom is one of many possible arrangements of just three smaller, simpler constituents, the proton, the electron and the neutron.

More recently we are finding that there are many more such "elementary particles" and they in turn can be described as complex arrangements of more basic things called quarks and gluons. Yet, we are far from finished. In this realm, explanation means being able to describe all the properties of complex things in terms of their basic constituents. All you need are the basic equations and the properties of the basic constituents. So, too, the Sages tried to make the system of halacha work this way, with the Thirteen Principles of Rabbi Ishmael, used to reason through the Torah and Talmud to answer questions. Rambam (Maimonides) also labored to present the mitzvot as a complete system with explanations of how everything followed from basic Torah precepts.

In physics, it is unclear whether this process bottoms out at some final, most basic building blocks, or keeps going, or perhaps this whole way of thinking about matter might be on the wrong track. It is a little reminiscent of the problem of infinite regress in describing what is holding up the (supposedly flat) Earth. One version is in Stephen Hawking's book "A Brief History of Time," as follows: "A well-known scientist (some say it was Bertrand Russell) once gave a public lecture on astronomy. He described how the earth orbits around the sun and how the sun, in turn, orbits around the center of a vast collection of stars called our galaxy. At the end of the lecture, a little old lady at the back of the room got up and said: 'What you have told us is rubbish. The world is really a flat plate supported on the back of a giant tortoise.' The scientist gave a superior smile before replying, 'What is the tortoise standing on?' 'You're very clever, young man, very clever,' said the old lady.

'But it's turtles all the way down!'"

Now, you might ask, where did these rules and behavior come from? The last 50 years or so, this is exactly the kind of question theoretical physicists are struggling with. Ideas you may have heard of like String Theory,

Quantum Gravity and Multiverses are the latest products of the imaginations of physicists. It is an adventure of the mind like no other. It defies expression in even the fanciest computer graphics and science fiction movies. These visual special effects come nowhere close to the weirdness of current theories of fundamental physics.

Explanation aside, there is a difference between the laws of physics and the laws of Torah. But before discussing that, I want to mention ice hockey. We have *chukim* (statutes) for ice hockey too. The lines on the ice determine where players can skate, relative to the puck, how many players are on the ice at any time, what constitutes a score, what is foul play, and so on. Some of these have an explanation or partial explanation, but most were just made up by some people a relatively short time ago. For example, there is a rule in ice hockey, the offside rule, which says a player may not cross the opposing blue line ahead of the puck. There is also an offside rule in soccer, but the field markings are different and the rule is somewhat different too.

Why are they different? Which one is "true" or "right"? I will venture to say simply that the rules of ice hockey make its identity, and distinguish it from soccer. If you want to play ice hockey you learn and follow the rules. We do, of course, make incremental changes in the rules, just as *halacha* evolves over time.

How is it that *halacha,* the derived rules of the Torah, can change with time?

There are two reasons. One is that the mitzvah system of the Torah is incomplete, even with the inclusion of the Oral Law. Many questions are not only not explainable in the Torah, but not even answered, except by "reading between the lines," taking account of the conditions of the community and our time in which we live. How do we do that? I don't know, but it is up to us, as it is written in *parashat Nitzavim,* The Torah is not in Heaven, it is ours to actualize as we see fit.

We decide if the laws of physics are true by measuring and observing. However, we have no similar way to determine if the rules of ice hockey are "true." They are what we made them. Torah, too, is prescriptive rather than predictive, so there is no way to do experiments to test if the Torah is "true". It is an unsolved problem. This is not about whether the Torah was handed down from God at Sinai. It is about what we make of it. For me, being an ice hockey player means I learn how to play, and I do play, at the level where I am comfortable. Being a Jew means I learn Torah and do mitzvot at the level where I am comfortable. Nothing could be better than that.

A Postscript

Sometime after writing this d'var Torah, I read the novel, "As a Driven Leaf," by Milton Steinberg. It is a fictionalized tale of the life of Rabbi Elisha ben Abuya, a Sage of the 4th generation of the *Tannaim,* about 110-135 C.E. Not much is found in the Talmud about Elisha, but he is well known for the incident which is claimed to be the breaking point at which he finally denies the existence of God and rejects the Torah (Chagigah 15b). A father asks his son to climb a ladder to fetch the eggs in a nest in a tree. The boy performs two important mitzvot, of which the Torah teaches one will be rewarded with long life, "Honor your father and your mother," and "Send away the mother bird before taking her eggs." In the process he falls off the ladder and dies. Elisha, witnessing this, takes it as proof that the Torah is not true, and becomes an apostate. Steinberg's work of fiction depicts in the character of Elisha a passionate lifelong search for Truth, for an understanding of the Torah and Judaism in terms of irrefutable and firm principles, rather than on faith. His model is Euclid's method for presenting geometry as a logical system in which everything known is derived from a few self-evident principles. To some extent this was also what his contemporaries were seeking in the debates and discussions recorded in the Talmud. The debate goes on, and Steinberg's account of Elisha might be seen as revealing Steinberg's own journey.

Since my childhood, when I began to learn science and mathematics, I too have been on this search. Logic and mathematical reasoning have been my guide and tools.

Nevertheless, there are questions that are simply not scientific questions, but ones for which the answers, if there are any, come from within. These are questions of values, what do we care about, what is important and what is not important. What will we make of our lives, what meaning does life have for us? To these questions, the Torah and the Jewish tradition can help us find answers.

One Sunday morning at my seventh grade Hebrew School class, we were discussing the idea of doing mitzvot (commandments). I explained to the students that I did not believe we get rewarded for doing mitzvot, but we should do them because they are the right things to do, that is our purpose, as civilized people. One student gave a dissenting view. She said, "Yes, there is no specific reward for doing a mitzvah, but when you are able to do it, you feel really good afterward." I was speechless.

Who Were the Tishbites?

Mary and Eric Horvitz hosted a Pesach Seder in the Spring of 2010 (5770), attended by Terry and me, Eric's family, including his Dad, who lives in Rockville Centre, New York (on the south shore of Long Island), where I grew up, and our friends Yuri and Zoe Gurevich. After welcoming Elijah the Prophet with the traditional song, someone asked what "Eliyahu HaTishbi" meant. Was he a "Tishbite," from someplace called "Tish," or was there some other explanation? Afterwards I did some searching. The email I wrote to Eric, reproduced here, reports my findings.

From: Ira Kalet

Sent: Monday, March 29, 2010 11:30 PM To: Eric Horvitz

Subject: Tishbite

Hi, Eric,

Thanks again from Terry and me for a wonderful seder.

Here is what I found. Please feel free to share it with anyone who might be interested, and with your Dad in particular.

There is a Wikipedia entry for "Tishbite." It is short.

Tishbite is a word used in the Bible to refer to Elijah (1 Kings 17:1, 1 Kings 21:17-28, 2 Kings 1:3-8, 2 Kings 9:36). The phrasing can be reworded as "Elijah the Tishbite of Tishbe in Gilead." The word is sometimes interpreted as "stranger," so that the verse might read "Elijah the stranger from among the strangers in Gilead." This designation is probably given to the prophet as denoting that his birthplace was Tishbe, a place in Upper Galilee (mentioned in the deuterocanonical Book of Tobit, Tobit 1:2). Josephus, the Jewish historian Ant. 8:13, 2), however, supposes that Tishbe was some place in the land of Gilead. It has been identified by some with el-Ishtib, a place 22 miles due south of the Sea of Galilee, among the mountains of Gilead.

What they refer to as "reworded" is actually a literal word for word translation of the Hebrew, "Eliyahu ha-tishbe mi-t'shavei gilad." The reason the word can be interpreted as "stranger" is that it comes from the root "yad-shin-bet," meaning "to sit," from which we get "yeshiva," where people sit and study, "yishuv," a settlement or settled region, "moshav," a cooperative farming community, like a *kibbutz* but with private homes and plots of land, and "toshav," inhabitant or settler. This also relates to "ger toshav," usually translated as "resident alien," not quite "stranger".

It's a stretch. It is *not* related to "stranger in a strange land," which is from Exodus (2:22) when Moses and Zipporah have a son they name "Gershom" (ger shom, stranger there). Hag sameach, and as John Ciardi used to say, "Good words to you".

Ira

Here is Eric's reply:

Dear Ira and Terry,

Great information below on Tishbite!

Thanks for coming by last night. We enjoyed spending time with you!

I've cc:'d my father so you can have a link to his centRE of operations in Rockville Centre!

Eric

Eric Horvitz

Who Were The Tishbites?

Later, I discovered a far fetched connection. Ice hockey fans, especially from Canada, will of course know that the nickname of the Montreal Canadiens ice hockey team is the "Habs." Being more of an amateur player than a fan, this puzzled me, so it was that around this same time, I looked for some history and was delighted to find the following, also from Wikipedia:

"Habitants were French settlers and the inhabitants of French origin who farmed the land along the two shores of the St. Lawrence Gulf and River in what is the present-day Province of Quebec in Canada. The term was used by the inhabitants themselves and the other classes of French Canadian society from the 17th century up until the early 20th century when the usage of the word declined in favour of the more modern "agriculteur" (farmer) or "producteur agricole" (agricultural producer). In English, the Montreal Canadiens team's main nickname is "the Habs," an abbreviation of "Les Habitants."

This conveys the same sense of reference to the "residents" or "settlers," the people who lived there, as in Hebrew.

So perhaps the Habs are an offshoot or descendent of the Tishbites.

The 1970s were the glory years of the Montreal Canadiens, with Ken Dryden as their goalkeeper, and among other legends of ice hockey, the great Jean Beliveau as their leader. The Habs have not been the dominant team they were in their greatest era, but hopefully a prophet will come and lead this group to victory once again.

Go Tishbites!

Short Story Writer

JAN • 62 •

Although I was known throughout school as one of the small band of math and science whiz kids, at the end of Senior year, my reputation took an abrupt turn in a very different direction. Our English teacher, Ms. Helen Grow, gave us our last assignment for the year, indeed the last assignment of high school for almost all of us, due Friday, one week before the end of school. The assignment was to write a short story, a work of fiction, with only one requirement. Ms. Grow provided five sentences from which we were to choose one, and use it as the first sentence of the story. Being the science and math geek, I thought I would write a science fiction style short story. I had read and enjoyed many such stories, by Isaac Asimov, Arthur C. Clarke, Poul Anderson, and many others. Night after night I thrashed my brain searching for a story idea. Nothing came. Thursday night, the proverbial night before the assignment was due, I had written nothing. I was scared. I had to turn in something, but what? Late that night, an idea struck like lightning. I cooked up a fantasy story based on a trip on the New York City subway some months earlier. Once the idea was clear, the narrative poured out like a flood. English class was the last period of the day, so I had time during lunch to rewrite my hastily scribbled draft (1961 no computers back then), so it could be turned in. As I copied it, my best friends Jim Ritter and Eric Marks, read the draft over my shoulder. They were incredulous. "Ira, you aren't really going to turn this in, are you? You will be expelled from school." But what choice did I have? I had to turn in something. After lunch my rough draft circulated among classmates throughout the school. By seventh period, probably half the Senior class had read it. Everyone feared for my future.

I turned it in. Ms. Grow took all our submissions home and on Monday when we were all back, she informed us that she had read all of them. "Some were good, some not so good," she said, and some, she said, were not actually stories. "But there was ONE…" My heart skipped a beat. Jim was right, I thought, I was going to get suspended or worse.

Here is my story. At the end I have appended Ms. Grow's evaluation, but of course you can judge for yourself.

Hobby
by Ira Kalet

A short story, written May 22, 1961 for Senior English class, taught by Miss Helen Grow, last assignment of the school year, South Side High School, Rockville Centre, NY

The woman was begging. She really was asking for it. In all my years on the subway, never until today did I encounter such a girl. Because of her, I was miles out of my way, here in the Bronx. I first noticed her at the Seventh Avenue stop. She stood beside me, peering out the front car window, as I did, into the onrushing tunnel.

"Pretty, isn't it?" she remarked softly, in an effort to communicate. Yet, to me, a veteran model railroader, it was pretty, and as I glanced at her I saw that she was attractive, too. She tried again to attract my attention.

"Have you ever been to Coney Island?"

"No," I replied, curtly. "I don't care for such nonsense." "How do you spend your free time, then?" she inquired. "I manage," I snapped.

"You're not very talkative, are you?" she tried once more.

At this I relented, and we sat down together, in the front car. As I spoke of my interest in model railroading, she rested her head on my shoulder, and I could see she wasn't listening. The momentum as the train came to a halt pressed her closer to me, and I slowly put my arm around her. She smiled approvingly. The train sped on, and we said little. I could feel her heart thumping, as rapidly, perhaps, as my own.

[On my paper at this point, Ms. Grow had written, "Why, Ira!"]

When we were far uptown, far from my destination in Brooklyn, she quietly whispered, "This is my stop."

"Must you go?" I pleaded. She beamed as she realized how successful she had been.

"You may walk me home, if you like," she replied, invitingly, and I, with my hand gripping hers, could not refuse. We drifted away from the teeming platform, toward and exit. Suddenly we were surrounded by daylight, and her pony-tail, waving in the gentle breeze, caught my eye. I released her hand, and once again placed my arm about her perfect figure. Unconscious of where I was going, I asked her name. "Nina," she answered, and drew nearer. My arm tightened around her waist.

"We turn here. It's another block," she explained. "And then what?" I inquired.

"And then we are at my house," she said.

"Stop playing games and answer my question!"

"What question?" she asked innocently. My arm relaxed, and I moved away.

"Well, I've got to get going," I glibly remarked. Now it was her turn.

"Must you go?" she pleaded. She pressed her enticing body close to me. "Would you like to stay with me for a while?" She caressed my neck as she spoke. The woman was begging and I stood there helplessly in her arms.

Throwing caution to the wind, I went in. We quickly walked through the modestly, but attractively furnished living room and into her bedroom. The walls were decorated with college pennants, the most prominent being Syracuse. The neatly made bed appeared unslept in, though I was convinced that it would soon be in use. She stood before me, breathing heavily. With each rise and fall of her sparsely covered chest, my heart beat wildly. Her arms slowly crept over my shoulders, and her soft lips drew near. I tightened my arms about her waist, and pressed her lips to mine. My vision blurred in that moment of ecstasy, and my head began to throb. Gently, surely, she caressed my neck and shoulders. Effortlessly, she removed her blouse, laying bare her exquisite bosom. Quickly shredding our remaining garments, we slipped into her bed. In one fleeting moment, I recalled where I was, and what had happened, but would not, in fact, could not, heed my better judgement. The moment was gone, and I was caught in a whirlpool of exotic passion.

I glanced at the clock on the wall. Four-thirty was too late for my intended visit. Beside me, Nina slowly opened her eyes. A vague frown crossed her lips, as I stood hesitantly by her bed.

"Well, now that you're satiated, why don't you get dressed and go," she snapped. I could not say I was not satiated, and thought it best not to ask if she wished to be paid… yet I hadn't expected that remark. I asked her last name.

"Why do you ask?" she retorted.

"I hope this isn't the last time we see each other," I answered.

"Do you really like me?" she asked, amused.

"Yes," I said.

"Why, that's the funniest thing I ever heard!"

"I don't understand."

"Look here." She showed me a picture of a blond boy with a beautifully formed nose. It had some writing on it.

"To dearest Nina, who inspires my basketball playing, from Paul," I read. "The greatest guy in the world," she said, a little wistful.

"But why… I mean… with me?"

"Oh, just a hobby of mine. You build trains; well, I ride them!"

Disgusted, I dressed and left. Nothing pleased me more than putting plenty of distance between us.

Since then I have given up model railroading, and taken up ham radio instead. It's a much safer hobby. Why, just the other day, I was talking, on the air, to a girl a few miles away who has the most seductive voice and, let me tell you, the woman was begging.

Ms. Grow continued, "there was one that was head and shoulders above all the rest, a truly great story…." Wew, I heaved a sigh of relief, someone else's story. I'm just going to get a bad grade, but graduate anyway.

Of course everyone wanted to know whose story it was. Yes, it was mine. Now I was really in shock. Here is what she wrote on the paper. "100. You're wasting your time with NaCl, H2SO4 and D. and Q. You can write short stories for a living."

Needless to say, I didn't take her advice. But it certainly put a different color on my reputation among my classmates, who until that point saw me as the shy math whiz. It was great fun to pop out of high school with a flourish.

Admissions & Detractions

A Tale of Two Cities
by Ira Kalet

> Written in 1971, as part of an application for admission to the
> University of Washington School of Medicine, to pursue an
> M.D. degree.

Once upon a time, in the lands just beyond, there was a city called
Gronkberg. It was a large city, nearly one million people, beset with the
usual problems, overcrowding, pollution, racial tension, unemployment
and hippies, to mention a few. Not the least of its problems was a serious
lack of doctors and medical facilities. Although there was a magnificent
medical school in the city it unfortunately was only big enough to admit
ten students each year. But the city of Gronkberg needed at least five hundred doctors, for disease was rampant, people were falling off their bicycles
and motorcycles and colliding with each other in their cars, other people
were shooting each other, and people were dying for lack of care. That year
the mayor appointed a commission to search for funds to expand the medical school of Gronkberg and if possible even build another one. The commission first spoke to the rich people of the city. But the rich people all felt
there was adequate medical care (and added that they certainly felt no obligation to pay for the well-being of the poor people of the city). The commission spoke to the working people and the poor people but because the

city taxes were so high they all could barely afford to pay their own medical bills, not to mention contributing to a medical school. Then the commission went to the city council to see where the tax money was being spent and to ask if the city council could help. But the city council was spending most of its money on a great complex of machinery to defend Gronkberg from enemy attacks. In particular, the city council was convinced that the neighboring city of Blonkberg was a dangerous enemy, that Gronkberg must be prepared to defend itself and if necessary even attack the city of Blonkberg. The commission members were very sad. They reported back to the mayor and the mayor reported to the medical school, where the admissions committee then got on with the business of choosing who would be the ten students.

By then they had received one thousand applications. About half the applicants were obviously well qualified, while the remainder were really not qualified. But the committee still had to choose ten from these five hundred well qualified people. They required the applicants to take a standardized "aptitude and achievement" test and they had the applicants compute and convert and recompute their grade point averages. Still the committee could not decide among one hundred or so remaining applicants, so the applicants were asked to write an essay. They wrote on all kinds of subjects. One wrote on John Donne's use of metaphysical metaphor. Another wrote on the significance of the philosophical foundations of the quantum theory. Another wrote on the psychological and sociological origins of the association of pink with girls and blue with boys. Another wrote a brief political analysis of the recent city council elections. The committee read the essays and chose the ten people.

This went on for several years. Meanwhile, the health situation had worsened. The infant mortality rate went up, and the poor and working people were dying or leaving the city in disgust. At first the rich people were not worried, but the garbage began to pile up and the sewers were not working. Other services failed because there were not enough people to keep them operating. Then rich people also began to contract diseases in great number and their hospital could not help them. Finally a delegation went to the city council imploring the city council to obtain help, even from their enemies in Blonkberg if necessary. A caravan was quickly assembled to go to Blonkberg for help. When they arrived in Blonkberg they discovered that Blonkberg was as devastated as their own city, for the Blonkbergians had made the same mistakes. They also had a huge defense machine and fewhad hoarded their money.

So both cities decayed and died.

> Moral: Money has been shown to be an effective decay-preventive agent that can be of significant value, but ONLY when used in a conscientiously applied program in support of training and regular professional care.

I was not admitted to the University of Washington School of Medicine for that year (or to any of the other medical schools to which I applied). However, Dr. Ben Belknap, the Director of Admissions at the UW School of Medicine, wrote a personal letter saying that the Admissions Committee's decision was based on my not having the minimum course requirements in chemistry and biology, and he suggested that I enroll in these classes and reapply. So I did. I took organic chemistry, physical chemistry and cell biology.

In the meantime in order to support myself and save some money for the (hopefully) coming ordeal, I obtained a job at Harborview Medical Center in the Microbiology Department, as a laboratory technician. It involved a rotation of one week day shift and two weeks of "swing" shift, 3:30 PM to Midnight. During the night shifts, the job involved checking in specimens from patients, and using the material to inoculate various kinds of agar growth media in Petri dishes, and making slides using the Gram stain technique. My day shift responsibilities varied but involved many different tasks to insure that the supplies were in place for use later, as well as helping to handle specimens that came in during the day.

One day as I was spending some hours stuffing small wads of cotton into the ends of glass pipettes and packing them into envelops for sterilization, the Director of the Laboratory, Dr. C. Evans Roberts, came by. After watching me for a few minutes, knowing my background, he slowly and dryly said to me, "I'm very glad to see how well we are utilizing the talent available to this laboratory." Subsequently, Dr. Roberts got me involved in a project to analyze some data he and associates had obtained on pyocine production and susceptibility in pseudomonas aeruginosa. This bacterial species can be a very dangerous and difficult problem as it often turns up as the infecting organism in hospital acquired infections. There are many different strains or variants, and by precisely classifying a particular infection, and others at the same time, it is possible to identify the source of the infection. I wrote a computer program to determine if the patterns of different strains' effects on each other could be used for such classification. It looked promising but we did not have time to complete the project.

When I was hired for the laboratory assistant job, the manager explained that she chose me because the other candidate had said he quit his last job after only a few months to go mountain climbing. Bonnie was herself an avid hiker and modest climber, but, she explained, they needed someone who would stay with the job at least a year. I told her that was highly likely since I am reapplying for admission to medical school and the timing seemed excellent. However, as in the previous year, I was not admitted by any of the medical schools to which I applied. So in early Spring I told Bonnie that my medical school plans had fallen through and I was resigning my position so that I could go mountain climbing.

As it turned out, one of the teaching assistants for the courses I took was also a mountain climber. We became climbing partners that Summer, and one of the most exhilarating climbs we did was the West Ridge of Mount Stuart, in the Cascades. Actually we got off route and onto the Southwest Face, where we climbed a more difficult section, not realizing where we were.

Nevertheless, we got to the summit in plenty of time, enjoying a bite to eat and an extraordinary view. As we talked, the conversation turned to recent history, and when I mentioned that I had previously worked at the Harborview Microbiology Lab, my climbing partner said, "Oh, yes, I applied for that job, but Bonnie told me she gave the job to someone else, since I had quit my previous job to go climbing, while the other candidate (guess who?) planned to go to medical school and was more likely to stay on the job for at least a year." We had a good laugh, and then began our descent down Ulrich's Couloir on the South side of Mt. Stuart.

I decided that this path was not for me. I turned to teaching, and then after some years, became involved in medical physics, returning to the University of Washington at first as a postdoctoral trainee, then as a member of the faculty in the Radiation Oncology Department, in the School of Medicine. One of the most amusing adventures of my career was serving for two years on the University of Washington School of Medicine Admissions Committee. It was indeed a (Groucho) Marxian experience not only to be a faculty member in the school that did not admit me as a student, but to be on the Admissions Committee as well.

Obituary

Ira Joseph Kalet
died on Saturday
February 21, 2015

Recently Ira wrote "What a strange world this world is. Sometimes I get so scared of what we make of it. Other times it seems not to matter at all because the world is infinite and what we do is a transient blip. And sometimes it seems one person can really change the world." Ira was one of those people who touched many lives and left this world a better place.

He survived by his wife of 41 years, Terry and their three sons, Nathan, Alan, and Brian. Ira hiked the cascades with his sons, sharing chocolate every few miles to keep them going, coached soccer teams and shared his love of music. Most importantly, he shared his love of Judaism as he blessed his sons every Shabbat. As his death approached he was able to bless his children and grandchildren Morrigan and Brandan Kalet one last time.

We would like to thank Dr. John Thompson and the team at the SCCA for helping Ira survive for 13 years with kidney cancer.

Dr. John Thompson

Many times he defied the odds to bounce back from seemingly impossible situations.

His last few weeks were filled with love. In a final prayer Ira wrote

"Dear God, thanks for being so good to me, but be sure to take care of family and everyone else who needs help."

Ira lived with intensity and tied not to waste a day.

Kalet Family Photos

Wedding of Ben and Millie Kalet

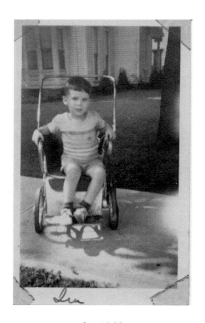

Ira 1946

Ira and Gloria about 1947

Ben, Ira, Hazel, Gloria, Stephen and Millie Kalet 1985

Ira and Terry 1973